UNIVERSITY OF
WOLVERHAMPTON
ENTERPRISE LTD.

Teaching Tomorrow

"Imagination is more important than knowledge."
(Albert Einstein, 1879-1955).

"The important thing is not to stop questioning."
(Albert Einstein, 1879-1955).

Teaching Tomorrow

Personal tuition as an alternative to school

John Adcock

Education Now Books
Nottingham, England
2000

© John Adcock
First published: 2000
ISBN: Hardback : 1.871526.46.9
      Softback : 1.871526.44.2

British Library Cataloguing in Publication Data:
A catalogue record for this book is available from
the British Library.

Cover design by:
Penelope Jane Randall

Published by:
Education Now Books
113 Arundel Drive, Bramcote Hills
Nottingham NG9 3FQ

Typeset and Printed by:
Adlard Print & Reprographic Services, The Old
School, Village Green, Ruddington, Nottingham,
NG11 6HH.

Contents

List of tables:

Foreword

This book is concerned with possibilities in the evolution of education. It argues that technological changes have provided the opportunities to reorganise fundamentally how education is provided. Such reorganisation is now necessary.

In recent years, every country with a Government Department for Education has earmarked increasing resources for the consideration and implementation of developments in *Information Communications Technology*. The impact on the means and methods of teaching and learning has already been considerable. Organisations and individuals with an interest in education have felt it necessary to keep abreast of ICT developments. So far we may have seen only the beginning of fundamental reforms in the way in which societies organise education. Schooling and the teaching/learning process may be about to change in the early years of the 21st century even more rapidly than they did in the same period of the 20th. This book argues that the time has come for the traditional school-based system of education to be tested for effectiveness and relevance, and that ICT developments have made such an examination viable.

As the General Secretary of the National Association of Schoolmasters Union of Women Teachers with 200,000 teachers in membership, from all four countries of the United Kingdom, I have seen the impact of new ideas in ICT on schools and colleges, and on the key element of teachers' work in the classroom. John Adcock, as a member of NASUWT for thirty years, has been in the forefront of radical thinking about the school system and ICT. His novel, *'In Place of Schools: a novel plan for the 21st century'* (1994), and his articles and essays have encouraged readers to consider what sort of future the education service might face. Some of his 'alternative' ideas - like that of *professional personal family group tutors* for all children - are controversial but deserve our careful attention.

While neither I nor NASUWT would necessarily subscribe to or support John Adcock's analysis, I have no doubt that in this book he makes an important contribution to the debate of *'where next and how'* in education. New ideas, such as those in *'Teaching Tomorrow'*, enhance the quality of that debate and it is one which should be joined by all those interested in the sort of society we are to develop.

Nigel de Gruchy,
General Secretary, NASUWT, Covent Garden, London.
26th July 1999

Preface

The institution

There is always danger in seeking to replace one of society's firmly established institutions with one that is radically different and largely untried. There is particular danger in proposing that the institution of school be jettisoned in favour of a family-based approach to the education of children: an approach which would mean that children would not attend any school-like assembly until they had passed their fourteenth birthday.

The danger is not, hopefully, that the proposer will be hanged, drawn and quartered for dissidence, but that in making criticism of school as an institution in society it might be read that it is individual pupils, parents or teachers who are under surveillance. That is not so. The school as a concept, in this case as a way of educating children, can be criticised over and above the people involved in its working. In the same way the hospital, prison or church can be rigorously scrutinised without detracting from the service provided by doctors, nurses, governors, warders, clergy and lay preachers. Similarly, no criticism of individuals or groups in schools or colleges is intended here. As one who taught in primary, secondary and higher education for 32 years I know how conscientious teachers are, how fully many parents support them, and how hard most children work. The point being made in this book is that if the institution were replaced, all this energy might be better used and the sum of human happiness increased.

Nor is it claimed that nothing is being done to promote the institution. Money is poured in: inspectors are appointed, class sizes are reduced, in-service training is given, the curriculum is revised, the importance of literacy is emphasised, Green Papers are distributed and computers are purchased by the truckload. The trouble is that this money might well be wasted unless the institution itself is examined rigorously. At the same time viable alternatives to the school could be considered, tried and tested. It is unfortunate that, as yet, there seems little inclination at a high level to look seriously and dispassionately at really radical alternatives despite worrying developments in various parts of our century-old school-based system.

Note: Throughout this book tutors are referred to as 'she' and children as 'he'. This is to avoid the tedious repetition of 'he or she', 'him or her', and 'his or hers'. It is not an indication that in future there will be no male tutors or female pupils.

1. A New Look

A change for the better

The promotion of literacy in the 1870s

Despite austere buildings, uninspiring interiors, harsh regimes, a restrictive curriculum, minimally trained teachers and meagre resources, the early state-controlled schools of the 1870s and 1880s did much good for many children and great good for some.

Those schools gave most of their conscripted pupils a modest degree of numeracy and a utilitarian level of literacy. Most children were taught to read for themselves; many were given access to printed information for the first time; some learned of the pleasures to be derived from literature, while a few, who had gifted, thoughtful teachers, gained a life-changing introduction to the arts and to the whole exciting world of new ideas. Although their classroom windows were set too high to give a view of life outside, those fortunate few had their eyes opened to an imaginary world of what had been and what might be.

But it is doubtful if that school-based concept of 'popular' education provided much in the way of human happiness. The system developed was one in which children of five to ten, and later, twelve years were taken from their homes to be instructed in buildings set apart from the wider community. They were taught in considerable numbers by persons largely unknown to them or their families. At that time such a system was, in all fairness, the only practical option open to governments intent on gaining, rapidly, a literate and numerate population. It is likely that the best was done with what was to hand.

That same system has been with us for over 125 years. The fundamental school-based structure of separate premises, halls and classrooms, hierarchical teaching staff, set school terms and hours and a state-provided, restrictive, inspected and assessed national curriculum are here today as strong as ever.

Yet, while almost everything else in Western society has changed beyond recognition, huge sums of money are spent on retaining this 19th century school-based system. Much more will be needed to take it from the 20th century into the 21st. The question has to be asked: "Will it be money well spent?"

9

Perhaps the time has come to take a wholly new look at what is being done with children's education for, despite growing expenditure, there are clear signs that parts of the system are failing. Some sixteen-year-old pupils still leave school eagerly in a semi-literate state, bullying is of great concern, and vandalism and truancy are commonplace. Parents desperately try to avoid sending their children to some schools and oversubscribe to others. Teacher disenchantment is demonstrated by the numbers seeking early retirement, by stress-related illness, by difficulties in filling some headteacherships, and by problems with the recruitment of talented young graduates. Sadly, the country has, for many reasons, watched a job which could be wonderfully exciting, personally rewarding and socially essential, being abandoned by many of those in post and declined by others who could offer much.

The state nevertheless persists with the notion that one day the school-based system will come good for all children, all parents and all teachers, and that if we wait a little longer, spend a great deal more money, inspect, legislate, and switch a few priorities, then all will be well: there is no need therefore to take seriously even the possibility of providing alternatives to school-based learning.

If there were available no alternatives to the school-based system this attitude would be understandable. 'Good' schools would have to be made better, and 'poor' schools helped to emulate them. But that is not the case: that is not the only course open.

Exciting alternatives have been around since the 1970s and 1980s: a hundred years after the first state schools were built. One has only to note how enjoyably, how effectively and how much children learn from radio, television, cassettes, personal computers and their own choice of reading to see powerful alternatives waiting in the wings to be sensibly and cautiously developed.

One such alternative approach to the teaching of children is developed in this book. While it is not the only idea that will be formulated in the 21st century, and while it is unlikely to appeal to all or be suitable for all, it is worthy of consideration by any government. A pilot scheme involving volunteer children, parents and teachers would not be difficult to organise or assess. One is outlined in Chapter 8, *A Pilot Scheme: Five requirements.* (page 151).

One alternative

The proposal is that from birth to his fourteenth birthday, each child will, with the ongoing guidance of a professional personal family tutor, be raised first within the family and then, from an approximate age of two years, be raised within the family *and* within the personal tutor's own group of twenty similarly-aged pupils.

Working with the child's parents, the personal tutor will construct an individual study programme for each of her twenty pupils. The programme will heed the child's changing needs, the parents' wishes, the availability of teaching materials and venues, and the tutor's professional assessment of what is best for the child. The tutor will have the same degree of professional responsibility for the educational wellbeing of the child within the family that the general medical practitioner has for that family's health care.

The tutor will work with seven others in a tutor panel: a kind of 'educational group practice'. The panel will cover, in two-year steps, the seven stages from birth to the fourteenth birthday of the 140 children in its ministration.

Tutors will have provided, from a central audio-visual education library, a mass of teaching material at every level of comprehension. Such material will be transmitted, on request, to any terminal at any time in any venue chosen by tutor or parent. It will be the reliable and ready availability of this material that will make individual study programmes viable and the new approach possible.

The curriculum followed will be slanted steeply towards the encouragement of peaceful, friendly and caring co-existence with other people. Rivalry, selfishness, competition and baseless pride will be discouraged. Love for others, patience, accommodation, thoughtfulness and co-operation will be to the fore: all these are qualities essential to peoples of all races and nations if the problems of the 19th and 20th centuries are not to be carried into the 21st and 22nd, and if the settlement of differences is to be negotiated, war rejected and the world's resources conserved.

In future this curriculum will need to be so slanted – and faithfully followed – however the child's upbringing is managed and whatever system of education is in vogue at the time. Such a vital curriculum, with its inherent sound social values will stand a greater chance of being readily accepted if it is taught at a personal level with professional help and within the family, rather than by stressed teachers each working with thirty children in a large school. These are personal values which have to be acquired by all individuals. They will be best taught by parents and personal tutors working with children in small groups aided by the huge resources of a controlled media and a long term enjoyable exposure to the humanising influences of literature, music and art.

In Western society's materially wealthy nations there are now wonderful opportunities for making a fresh start. But in those countries many families and schools are in crisis already. There is not much time. Blatantly radical, practical proposals, such as the one offered in this book, which see family life and the education of children as a healthy entity, need serious consideration. In that sense, teaching tomorrow has to begin today.

2. Changing Times

1. Yesterday's legacy

Elementary education

During the 1870s and 1880s industrialising countries developed systems of elementary education that would ensure functional literacy and numeracy. This call for entire populations to be competent in the basics of reading, writing and arithmetic came, in the main, from five areas of 19th century life.

First was that of industry and commerce: the whole world of work. With growing complexity in manufacturing processes and increasing sophistication in trade, something more was required of workers than hands on shovels and counting on fingers. Rapidly developing markets in Europe and North America forced each industrialising country to make an urgent examination of its educational provision. As the world of work changed, the competence of the workforce had to change with it.

Second was the slow but steady progression of democracy. This developed alongside the increasing complexity of national and local government bureaucracy and the attendant increase in legislation. There was the need to maintain law and order in the spreading, heavily-populated urban areas. This all called for citizens who could read and comprehend, work out wages, taxes and prices, and have some idea of what they voted for in elections and what the laws passed by their representatives meant for them in everyday life.

Third, the churches – long to the fore in the elementary education of working-class children – sought a literate population able to read the Bible and understand its teachings. Organised religion – so long a power in most societies – was at a turning point. The contentious work of some scientists, and the writings of non-believers and agnostics, seemed to throw doubt on the underlying concepts of the churches' message and to question the basis of their authority. The future of church schools in countries such as Britain, and the teaching of religious knowledge generally, was uncertain.

Fourth, a widening band of social reformers saw the acquisition of literacy and numeracy by lower social groups as a precursor to further education and to greater equality of opportunity in later life. Not only did they see education as a means of alleviating poverty by providing employment, but they saw it as a way of releasing the latent talent of the children of the poor. It was also necessary if the in-built restrictions to national development brought about by nepotism and patronage were to be challenged effectively.

Fifth, many of those who appreciated the value of literature in their own lives wanted all young people to enjoy not only the masterpieces of the past but the novels, poems and plays emanating from the growing number of able, perceptive, free-thinking contemporary writers. With the advent of mass printing, low cost newspapers and magazines, and the provision of free public lending libraries, different and exciting perspectives on life could be disseminated widely. Social reformers, articulate and well-organised, thought the vicarious experiences made possible through literature would offer insights to alternative lifestyles to those born without a privileged background. They visualised the humanising qualities of literature enriching not only their own lives but those of millions of others. Western society itself, they thought, would be much improved for that: all children must therefore be taught to read, to understand what they read, and to reflect on the new ideas inherent in that reading.

Although the fifth area was seen by some as the most praiseworthy, it was not seen in that way by most of those demanding universal literacy. Nor was a love of literature for its own sake the most important reason for the spread of schooling to all children. Unfortunately that fifth area, the simple enjoyment of literature and a realisation of what it could teach about life, does not seem to be the main reason for encouraging literacy today. In most developed countries, now as in the past, the justification for heavy expenditure on the basic education of children is the maintenance of economic competitiveness in the world and, until recently, in the provision of a vital weapon against nations having alien social systems such as fascism, capitalism, socialism or communism.

Thus, for a variety of reasons, the late 19th century saw the first of a series of education acts passed by various governments. These paved the way for compulsory, school-based education for all children between the approximate ages of five and twelve. From the time of these early education acts and until the outbreak of the First World War in 1914 in Britain and the Commonwealth and 1917 in the USA this basic provision was establishing itself in all industrialised states. The school-based system was secured.

This system legalised the daily removal of children from their homes so that they could be taught for scheduled periods of time in specially-constructed and publicly-maintained buildings known as 'schools'. In these places a standardised curriculum was followed and the soundness of its inculcation was externally assessed. The teachers responsible for the work were not chosen by parents; children were allocated to schools and classes by educational administrators many of whom lived and worked at a considerable distance from the schools. The teachers were not members of the child's family and often knew little of the family's intimate background. The teacher's principal role was that of paid instructor. As such, it could not be regarded as a professional one and its relatively low status was set for many decades ahead.

From the 1870s parents and members of the child's extended family could, in all fairness, claim that they were no longer solely responsible for their child's upbringing. The resultant division of responsibility for a child's wellbeing – between the family on the one hand and the state school on the other – has been with us ever since, as have the repercussions.

Even so, the advances made were a tribute to the peoples of those times and indicate a steady level of change that can be traced to the first Industrial Revolution in England in the late 18th and early 19th centuries, and to a second revolution in science, technology, medicine and exploration in the later decades of the 19th and the early decades of the 20th centuries.

In the 1870s the need to develop universal schooling was urgent and it was to be a massive undertaking. A start had to be made with the money granted and the materials and ideas available to the developers of the system at that time. Any system had to be a compromise as it had to be acceptable to conflicting political and religious views, and be within tight economic reins. It had to make social demands that were within the tolerance range of the general, unschooled population.

There was not a wholehearted welcome from all the families whose children were to be compelled to attend the schools; there was no precedent for such con-scription, and the loss of any child's earnings from employment or of its labour within the home was a matter for concern for many families – and perhaps still is today.

Given this, it is remarkable that any system of universal schooling got off the ground at all, and the pioneers deserve praise. No generation since has taken an equivalent leap in promoting popular education: changes that have followed have been built on the original work of those pioneers. The fact that such work may now be outdated is no more their fault than the obsolescence of the steam engine, sailing ship or stage coach is the fault of their once-enterprising design-ers and builders.

To obtain quickly, and within a parsimonious budget, the required level of literacy in a rapidly-rising child population there was no alternative to the school-based system. It was a system that mirrored the mass production meth-ods of the industries in which many of the children's parents were employed. The labour-intensive, standardised and routine work of the factories and mills provided an obvious model for the mass teaching of children. Not only was the organisational practice already there as an example, but it had been accepted into 19th century life. People were flocking from rural areas to join in. The new schools would not only teach children, they would supervise them while parents were at work. Both services were important then and still are today even though the 'from home to work' trend has been reversed as more parents work at home for some or all of their working time.

The pioneers of universal schooling faced a situation where many parents were illiterate or semi-literate. Such parents would have been incapable of teaching their children to read and write even if they had the time, desire and energy to do so. Their housing was unsuitable for any level of formal teaching and they lacked the most basic of teaching materials. It is difficult to comprehend now how little people then had.

Pioneers faced ignorance on the part of the general population. Children were accustomed to poor food and clothing, minimal health care, little privacy, little mobility and low expectations of life. Children's knowledge of the world was restricted to what they could learn of their immediate neighbourhood and what could be provided by family, peer group and church. Travel was limited, myths, legends and superstitions abounded.

Seen in another way, they lacked the books, magazines, radio, television, video recorders, cassettes, computers, disks, the Internet, telephones and travel so common today and so readily taken for granted by millions of children in many Western nations.

In those circumstances the 19th century school, restrained as it was, nevertheless had much to offer. A school which had imaginative teachers who were able to pass on their own interests in music, literature and art must have been a veritable godsend to their lucky pupils. But how many such schools and teachers were there?

Generally, as a national institution, the state elementary system was joyless. Standards of instruction in each school and how well the prescribed syllabus had been 'learned' were periodically checked by managers, governors or itinerant inspectors. The duration of their visits was short and the objectives of their enquiries limited. Nevertheless such visitations were often feared by low-status, insecure staff. In Britain, for a time, the level of teachers' pay was determined partly by the findings of such inspections: 'payment by results'. Comparisons with today's (1999) position in Britain are far more than just 'interesting'.

Thus, by 1900, in most parts of the developing world, law-supported removal of children from their homes to neighbouring schools was well established, as was the tendency to define education in terms of the instruction given by teachers in those compulsorily-attended schools. Children's early development was influenced more and more by unrelated adults working outside the ambit of the family. The child was conditioned by the instillation of standardised knowledge within a restrictive, rigid regime. He was well prepared to undertake, largely without question, a lifetime of routine work in a mechanised and impersonal society.

It is tempting to ask whether, if they could have foreseen the scale of the changes that were to take place in society in the next hundred years, these mass-education pioneers of the 1870s and 1880s would have formulated the school-

Figure 1. Comparative events, 1870-2000

	World	Technology	Education
1870			Promotion of literacy
	Franco-Prussian War.	Suez canal opened	Elementary Education Acts
	U.S.A. centenary	Darwin's *Descent of Man*	School-leaving age: 10
1880	Anglo-Boer War.		Compulsory schooling for all
	UK occupies Egypt		Payment by results
		Daimler petrol engines	
1890			School-leaving age: 11
	Demand for widening		
	of franchise		School-leaving age 12
1900	Death of Queen Victoria	Zeppelin trial flights	Local education authorities
			formed
	Old age pensions begin	Bleriot's Cross-Channel	Balfour Education Act.
1910	Chinese Republic formed	flight	Secondary schooling for
	First World War 1914-18		some children
	Russian Revolution: USSR		School-leaving age: 14
1920			
	UK General Strike	Popular radio broadcasts	Burnham Committee on
	Votes for women		teachers' salaries
1930	World financial crisis		
	World depression	Radar developed	
	Second World War 1939-45		Wartime evacuation of city
			schools
1940	Battle of Britain		
	Defeat of fascism	Jet engine developed	1944 Education Act
	Indian independence	Atomic bomb used	School-leaving age: 15
1950	Devaluation of £		Selection for grammar,
	Suez War	Hydrogen bomb developed	modern & technical schools
		Popular TV broadcasts	3-year teacher-training
1960			Equal pay.
	Moscow Test Ban Treaty	Man in Space	Open University founded
	Devaluation of £	Man on Moon	Comprehensive schools
1970			
	UK joins Common Mkt		School-leaving age: 16
	First UK woman premier	North Sea gas and oil	
1980	Falklands conflict	Personal computers	Local management of schools
	Collapse of USSR	Mobile phones	National curriculum,
		Video recorders	testing, inspection.
1990	Mgt Thatcher resigns	Channel Tunnel	
	Gulf War	Internet, digital TV	Bonus payments for teachers
	Iraq crisis	Millennium Dome	Promotion of literacy

Dates and events are approximate and for illustrative purposes only.

based system in the way they did. Probably they would, for not only did they have to use the only resources available to them then but, given their brief, they saw no reason to depart from the school-based example already to hand in the form of church schools or in private institutions for the privileged. Indeed, to provide something different might have been interpreted as the state offering something inferior to children of the lower classes.

Further, the concept that all children should, in the 1870s, be offered an education that would make them literate and numerate was, in itself, revolutionary. The notion was quite sufficient to be going on with for those who were to pay for such change through their local and national rates and taxes.

Already some feared that an 'educated' working class might 'get above itself' and that it might begin to question traditional values or to raise its material expectations unrealistically at the expense of the society's wealthier groups. Another worry for some was the realisation that the socially steadying influence of the established church would be weakened if, as was to prove to be the case, many of the new schools were to be secular in character. There was no need to take on board as well the extraordinary alternative views of educational free-thinkers, social reformers or philanthropists.

However, there was some comfort in the knowledge that by massing working-class children in separate buildings for fixed periods under the control of basically-trained teachers who were themselves from the working and lower-middle classes and who were appointed and supervised by local and central government committees and inspectors, the children would be observed, disciplined and trained for much of the time. They would, in other words, be out of mischief and out of sight.

The school system that emerged did not disappoint, and that fundamental regime, although modified and humanised, is the one we use today. It is perhaps our most potent legacy from the Victorian era.

2. Today's choice

A different world

Education is still regarded by many people as a person's preparation for full-time employment in a lifetime occupation, much as it was in the quite different social and economic era of the late 19th century.

How dramatically dissimilar the late 1990s are from that earlier time, and how inappropriate the old school-based system of education might be for the present generation of children and those who follow, should cause concern.

If some of the educational pioneers of the 1870s could be transported to the 1990s they would think they were on a different planet. Little in terms of buildings, communications, medicine, food, dress, transport, leisure, living standards or behaviour would make sense.

But one institution still visible in the 1990s, which might bring the comfort of familiarity to uneasy time travellers would be the school. Much there would not have changed. For while the second industrial revolution, in the 19th century, brought about a corresponding revolution in education by introducing free and compulsory schooling for all, no such initiative has followed the third. School-based education has been retained when all the technological indications are that it is no longer needed and may even be counter-productive in terms of satisfying the real needs of children and the changed society in which it works. It is as if nations have decreed that a school-based system will be kept, come what will, regardless of the economic cost to themselves or of the personal cost to some of society's most vulnerable members.

It would, of course, be absurd to claim that individual schools have not changed in 125 years. In some countries changes have been greater than in others, and, generally, changes affecting very young children have been more radical and beneficial than those made for other groups. Many changes have been for the better and have affected pupils, parents and teachers in large numbers.

Many children now find much in the modern classroom that is interesting, varied, enjoyable and worthwhile. Many appreciate the hard work done by conscientious teachers and respect them for it. Others miss the facilities offered by the school when, for considerable periods each year, it is closed.

Many children attend well-run schools and are highly motivated by caring, skilled teachers who enjoy their teaching and know its value. All this is often done to the satisfaction of parents who prize what is being offered and are keen to assist the school with time, money and ongoing support. Some will even move catchment areas to ensure a place in a favoured school so highly do they regard the work being done there.

My own daughters gained much from their schools, and now my four grand-daughters attend well-run schools in different parts of the country. Their work is stimulating, diverse and carefully gauged. They like to bring work home to show their parents and grandparents who are happy with the children's schooling. Teachers are ready to talk about their work, explain their teaching methods, and suggest ways in which parents can help. These are not isolated cases. Great good is being done in thousands of schools every day.

But, while no-one could deny the benefits accruing to many children who attend school, it would be wrong to hold that all is well. There are serious problems, some of which seem to worsen every year. These can result in some children gaining little from their schooling except perhaps a knowledge of their personal inadequacies and of their peer group's low rating in society. If this is really the end result of ten years of schooling it might be argued that those children could have been better served by not attending school at all. Much heartache could have been saved. It might be suggested that almost any alternative would have been better and that a great deal of money has been spent to no avail.

It would be a damning indictment of parts of a system which has been in operation for 125 years if it were to be shown that it is still being run in such a way that it is, with some young people, doing more harm than good. Such a situation would be impossible to defend in any country at any time. No child should be compelled to attend school and then find that he gains little or nothing from it.

Certainly there are difficulties faced by teachers and students. Problems in today's schools which should worry everyone include:

- Bullying: both physical and psychological. The full extent is not known.
- Indiscipline: this may be due to poor teaching, poor management of the school, or poor relationships between pupil and teacher; or, on the other hand, it could be due to children whose home backgrounds have helped to make them unmanageable anywhere and antagonistic towards teachers and other people 'in authority'.
- Truancy: serious in some areas, and sometimes ignored to avoid further disruption in the school.
- Exclusion: offers no real solution, and is given media publicity which can harden anti-school attitudes, anger parents, and lower teacher morale.
- Harassment: difficult to prove if cunningly pursued; it can be directed at teachers as well as pupils and members of their families.
- Vandalism: although now widespread in both city and rural areas, schools in urban localities are often targeted and arson is not uncommon.
- Low achievement: while illiteracy and innumeracy at age 16 are problems that make the headlines, it seems likely that many children could achieve far more than they do in those and other areas of the curriculum.

- Anti-authoritarianism: this, again, is not restricted to school life, but for teachers, dependent on a modicum of authority to do their work, it can cause work-related stress for them and time-wasting for their pupils.
- Violence: the worst cases of assault make world news, but 'minor' incidents and the associated fears of many children and teachers often go unreported.

All the points above – and others – have a detrimental effect on the pupils' and teachers' work. In excess, or in combination, they can lead to stress-related illness, lack of pupil progress, disillusionment, and thousands of requests by teachers for early retirement from their chosen occupation. There is reluctance to enter the profession at all and difficulty in filling headteacher vacancies.

But this is not all. Teachers have never been accorded the full professional status enjoyed by practitioners in other skilled occupations such as medicine, dentistry, architecture, accountancy, the church and the law. While some of the blame for this must lie with teachers themselves because of their historical unwillingness or inability to press for or accept a single, wholly self-governing professional body, much blame lies within society.

It is true that, in the UK at least, progress towards a higher status for teachers was made in the late 1960s and 70s with the arrival of longer training, all-graduate entry, ongoing in-service training, and some notable 'catch-up' pay awards. But the progress has not been continuous and is far from complete.

In fact the reverse is probably the case. Early indications from a British government 'green paper' (the name for a consultative document) of December 1998 are that the required 'giant step' to *full* professional status is unlikely to be taken. Such a step will come about only if the state-controlled, hierarchical, expensively-inspected school-based system is abandoned and teachers are given professional rights and responsibilities in deciding what is taught to each child, and how and why and when it is taught, together with the opportunity for frequent direct consultation with parents. As a corollary, teachers would be accountable for the results which follow from their decisions on what is taught and be answerable to their clients and to their single, governing professional body. But even after 125 years of state schooling a fully self-regulating profession for teachers in which they control entry is a long way off. The bulk of teachers are still 'assistants' and are confined to the classroom. They have:

- Pupils allocated to them, in batches, by others.
- A curriculum to follow which is, (in the UK), laid down nationally by people far removed from the individual pupil, parent and teacher.
- A syllabus to teach related to a standardised curriculum which is geared to supposed national needs and not necessarily to the child's personal needs as seen by his parent and teacher.
- Set standards to reach, at different ages, with their pupils.

- An externally imposed inspection service.
- A hierarchical structure within the school which still ranks class-teaching work at a relatively low level.
- Little direct unrestricted and sustained contact with pupils' parents.
- A prescribed timetabling system which can be frustrating, restrictive and arbitrary in the planning of professional work.
- External control of the length of the school lesson, day, week, term and year.
- Influential persons, appointed by others, some of whom may be non-teachers and professionally unqualified, who affect their work.
- Little guaranteed clerical, secretarial or auxiliary support when it is needed.

Far from helping in this matter, government action over the past twenty years, including new legislation and additional requirements, has hastened the decline of teaching as a professional calling and detracted from its attractiveness as a career. The more hopeful Sixties have given way to the increasingly gloomy and stressful Seventies, Eighties and Nineties. But this scenario is not one created by teachers bemoaning their fate. Concern about the condition of education in the country is widespread and may well be in other countries, too.

The most cursory reading of any issue of *The Times Educational Supplement* (Britain's leading newspaper dedicated to education) will indicate unease in many fields at every level. But the really worrying aspect is that most of the issues raised have been around for decades and were familiar to teachers such as myself who began work in the 1950s. For instance:

- Teacher shortages and problems with recruitment.
- Teacher-dissatisfaction not only with the amount of salary paid but with the salary structure and the way the money is allocated.
- Concern about literacy levels and uncertainty and argument about ways of teaching children to read.
- Concern that schools which get a 'bad name' often get worse because of that naming and the tendency of parents and teachers to avoid those schools.
- Concern about truancy levels.
- Concern about children with learning difficulties.
- Teacher-anxiety about inspection systems and the effects inspection can have on the professional status of teachers as a whole.
- Concern that many parents never visit schools to discuss their children's progress and that these parents are often the ones it would be most helpful to see.
- Knowledge of the wide variation in educability levels at infant school age.
- Knowledge that parental help can enhance a child's learning.
- Awareness of the special needs of pupils and teachers working in socially-deprived areas, both urban and rural.

- Realisation that life-enriching non-examination subjects in examinations such as the old School and Higher School Certificates, Matriculation, 'O' and 'A' level G.C.E., C.S.E., and the highly unpopular 11 plus, suffered because they were either not set, or not entered for, or not sought (on certificate) by prospective employers or institutions of further education.
- Knowledge of the importance of citizenship in a child's education..
- Awareness of the lack of physical resources in schools.

Also worrying is the fact that despite the passing of fifty or a hundred years and the employment of a small army of relatively highly-paid civil servants, politicians, academics, inspectors and advisors, these problems are still with us – some have got worse – and that many children are losing-out as a consequence. In fact, as with disputes in such areas as methods of teaching reading, setting and streaming, much seems to go round in a circle and then start all over again. This can breed cynicism, indifference or despair.

Perhaps it is simply common sense which is lacking. Perhaps it does not need a series of committees, green papers, or a bevy of surveys to point out much of what is wrong. Any intelligent, observant, caring parent or classroom teacher can see where the difficulties lie and what causes them. And their 'on the spot' suggestions for remedies are likely to be as efficacious as those of the more distantly placed, deep-probing, slow-working experts.

But if, despite all that is being done by many thousands of well-intentioned people in many areas and at many levels of the education service the problems persist and, in some cases get worse rather than better, then it could be the school, i.e. the school-based system of teaching children, which is failing. It is the institution that is at fault, not the people trying to make it work. It may be that the school, for many children, parents and teachers, has outlived whatever usefulness it had. It may be the very existence of the school as we have come to know it that is the major obstacle to the solving of many of the problems.

For a significant proportion of children, parents and teachers an alternative to the school would be helpful and attractive. For some such an alternative may be urgently required. But the very notion of moving-on from the school to something different causes pain in many quarters. There are frantic scratchings in the sands to make holes for heads of many sizes. But alternatives to the schools are already here and can be explored. Questions need to be asked about the existing school-based approach and about our insistence on its continuance. For instance does the school-based approach to child rearing:
- Enhance the happiness of all children?
- Help to protect children from ill-treatment within the family?
- Protect children from being bullied by peers?
- Enable parents to play a full part in their children's education?

- Enable teachers to use their talents to the full?
- Give good value for money?
- Help children to become conscientious, industrious, caring citizens?
- Lead children to a lifelong enjoyment of music, drama, literature and all the other arts?

There are no clear-cut answers to these questions. To each the answer could be "Some schools do, some schools don't." Or, "For some children, 'Yes', and for some children 'No'." Or, it could be that some schools in the system help many children a lot, some help a few a little, and others do precious little for anyone.

If that is the case, it is another reason for the school-based system to be examined, fairly-assessed, and its future role determined, and then for alternative systems to be considered, tried and judged. There could be room in wealthy, developed nations such as Britain and the U.S.A. for more than one approach to children's education and for several systems to run alongside each other.

A further test is to ask to what extent the current situation is (i) meeting the needs of the children and parents for whom the schools are provided; (ii) meeting the needs of the teachers who work in them; (iii) meeting the needs of the state which finds the money required. How relevant is what is happening to the wellbeing of the four parties involved: children, parents, teachers and state?

For instance how far can the school-based system satisfy all children's needs for:

- Developing character and personality.
- Love, security, understanding.
- A feeling of self-confidence, and of being useful and needed.
- Being shown how to help others.
- Being helped to conform to, and understand the need for, acceptable social behaviour.
- Assurances that parents and teachers are working together for their welfare.
- Being taken out of their immediate environment to see how others live and how other people interest themselves.
- Being shown what other areas of their country are like.
- Being introduced to a lifetime of useful, absorbing activities that will become increasingly important as life work-patterns change.

Or the needs of parents for:

- Help in acquiring the many skills of child-rearing.
- Feeling that they are an important, integral part of the child's education.
- Having a known, trusted professional to turn to when family difficulties arise.
- Relief, periodically, from the strain or ties of raising young children.

- A large multi-facility local community resource centre where other parents and teachers can be met and where leisure activities, educational opportunities and other interests are available for lengthy periods *every* day.

Or the needs of teachers for:

- Knowing that they are properly valued for the work they do.
- Knowing that they are, professionally, in control of their work and responsible both for what they do and for the effect their work has on children.
- Feeling that their expertise has been used fully and that others have benefited from its use.
- Realising that the immense resources of information technology are available to them daily on demand.
- The assurance that they are working with and within each pupil's family.
- The assurance given by membership of a single, strong professional body.

Or the needs of the state (or society) for:

- Citizens who understand the need for minimum fair and sensible laws and who are, therefore, ready to abide by them.
- Citizens who are able to use their increasing leisure time constructively.
- Citizens who see themselves as important members of the workforce.
- Citizens who become involved in community work and social activities.

In view of its apparent inability to meet the needs of sizeable groups in society it is remarkable that the national, school-based system has lasted so long in so many countries. The system is extensive and expensive and requires the force of law to sustain it. It is true that in the UK and USA it is not mandatory for children to attend school provided they are being educated competently in other ways; e.g. taught adequately by parents or tutors at home. But the bulk of the population thinks that school attendance at set times on 200 days a year *is* compulsory. Attendance officers are employed and recalcitrant parents appear in court to be admonished or fined with attendance orders served upon them.

Thus, with the abolition of national service, conscription or the draft for duties in the armed forces, the only remaining places at which citizens' long term attendance is obligatory are prisons, asylums for the seriously mentally ill, and the nations' schools.

In proposing alternatives to the school-based system it has to be queried why the present system remains in place. Why, when over a century of unprecedented social and technological change has produced a freer way of life for adults, does compulsory childhood education stay firmly in place, and why, in its fundamental school structure, has the system been so little altered?

The reason cannot be lack of viable alternatives. Technology has made possible attractive ways of offering children individualised teaching which is not school-dependent. The necessary ideas, techniques and funding are available already. What is lacking is the will enthusiastically to examine these alternatives and, unlike what has happened already in other areas of life, to challenge basic assumptions: in this case assumptions made about children's education. "The important thing is not to stop questioning," urged Einstein. With regard to schools we have hardly started.

Reasons for such reluctance to question are numerous and powerful. Possible reasons are:

- An unwillingness or inability to accept that society has changed so greatly within a normal life span.
- A lack of appreciation either of the extent of such change or that such change is ongoing, i.e. that a 'state of change' is now the norm and that any period of tranquillity is very much the exception and likely to be shortlived.
- The supposition that, despite all else that has happened in society, children can be taught more or less the same things, in the same ways, at the same times and in the same places by the same people and for the same reasons. Such sameness and continuity are soothing to those apprehensive of change or nostalgic for the past.
- A belief that little is really wrong with those traditional schools which were once attended by most adults, and that where necessary things can be put right by a few minor adjustments and the spending of a little extra money. Radical change, with its attendant discomforts, is therefore unnecessary.
- Low expectations of what education can do: schools are doing their best to do what they are required to do, which is largely to inculcate knowledge that will be helpful eventually in passing examinations, securing jobs, and instilling in children a modicum of discipline.
- The widely-held view that schooling *is* education and vice-versa. This is a view so deeply entrenched in Western culture that many find it impossible to envisage a society without schools, or a process of education that does not involve schools.
- A limited appreciation of the potential of the electronic media and information transmission processes and, or, a fear of their extension.
- An inability to appreciate the liberating, exciting role that could be played by the media in childhood education, in family lives and in teachers' work.
- A fear of escalating costs if the school-based system were to be replaced in whole or in part by a radically different alternative.
- The thought that there is no guarantee that the replacement will be better even if there were consensus on what the word 'better', in this context, means.
- The thought that an alternative system might be worse than the existing one: "Better the devil you know..."

- A need for parents to be relieved (by a school) of the demanding company and requirements of young children.
- A need for parents to have their children safely supervised while they themselves are at work or are following their own interests.

For these reasons, and others, the school-based system continues to dominate the educational scene to such an extent that there is a reluctance *even to examine* radical alternatives.

Yet, as the changes to many aspects of life are seen to be both ongoing and accelerating, the school-based system seems likely to become less and less appropriate for future generations of children. It will be less efficient in terms of what might be done, and its continuing existence will be increasingly difficult to justify. Young people, more aware of the potential of the electronic media, and more conversant with travel, will less readily accept that education should remain the prerogative of the static school and its schoolteachers. When that stage is reached the school will be beyond mere modification: mere modification will not satisfy those many perceptive pupils, parents and teachers who can see the power and advantages of carefully thought-out, properly controlled and personally tutored media-based alternatives, and of varied venues for study.

At the end of the Second World War (1939-45 for Britain, 1941-45 for the U.S.A.) most countries, including Britain, had the praiseworthy aim of providing a much better, free and appropriate education for all their children: it was to be as good as each country could afford. But the well-intentioned efforts of all those people charged with its provision may have been thwarted because their proposals had to be made within the confines of the school itself. The very institutionalised structure they were trying to enlarge and improve upon was restricting them in what they could do. Their equally well-intentioned successors are still, over fifty years later, unable to break free of the persuasion that education *is* school. Their efforts, similarly, will be to limited effect.

But now, and without prejudice to any person or group, there is a strong case for examining alternatives. It is hard to accept that, with all the social and technological changes that were made in the seventy years from 1870 to 1940, and again and to a much greater extent in the sixty years from 1940 to today, there is now no better way of preparing children for adult life than by congregating them in classrooms for 200 days a year for eleven years or more.

3. Tomorrow's opportunity

Three directions

In the future, childhood education could move in one of three directions:

1. The retention of the 125-year-old school-based system.

2. The abandonment of that system, with parents being asked to educate their own children as they see fit.

3. The introduction of an alternative school-free system in which parents are encouraged to work with professional tutors in the provision of a personalised education for each child.

1.   The first possibility is the retention of schools. The aim would be to improve all schools by keeping the laudable features of those considered 'best' and bringing all the others up to those standards. Full use would be made of teacher dedication, parental support, sound management, community involvement, fine physical resources, varied approaches to learning and corporate activities. The aim would be to provide an effective preparation for adult life. Some schools already offer this and, if the school-based system is to be retained, these attributes would need to be made available to all children at all schools.

But it is doubtful whether the system can produce universal excellence or anything like it. There are difficulties as of now in meeting current standards in some areas, standards which, even in official eyes, may be unacceptably low. It would be a supreme optimist who would envisage all children and their families benefiting greatly from the school-based system. Certainly that seems unlikely in the foreseeable future.

Already there exist behavioural problems, teacher disillusionment, deteriorating buildings, vandalism, family breakdown and competition for children's attention from the media. It seems likely that these problems will intensify.

If governments persist with a school-based system in these circumstances they will be forced into a policy of containment if a system-breakdown, beginning in vulnerable centres, is to be avoided. Such a policy might include:

- A more rigorous and increasingly frequent testing of pupils.
- A more sophisticated system of rewards and penalties.
- The tighter enforcement of attendance law.
- The provision of reformatory schools for persistently misbehaving pupils.
- 24-hour surveillance of school premises by police or school security guards to check vandalism and react quickly to arson.

- A more severe regime for the inspection of schools and teachers' work and the dismissal of those teachers thought *by the inspectorate* to be incompetent.
- Considerable reliance on 'payment by results' with salary reductions for poorly-performing teachers and ever-higher bonuses for those who teach best what the government deems should be taught.
- Early retirement, without pension enhancement, of those thoughtful, imaginative and creative teachers who are unwilling to conform to ill-advised central edicts because they have at heart the personal interests of their pupils.
- More generous stress counselling for teachers in those schools where tension is especially high, and the offering of similar services to pupils who are at risk of developing school-related nervous disorders such as school phobia, and to their concerned parents.
- Protection of teaching staff from abusive or violent pupils or parents, with substantial financial compensation for physical or psychological injury.
- The rights and responsibilities of parents to be made legally binding in a contract which requires (i) agreement between parent and school before admission is granted to a pupil and (ii) compliance with the contract if the child is to remain at that school.
- Increased representation of parents and teachers on school governing bodies and greater responsibilities for these bodies.

The basis of some of this 'containment' policy is already in place in schools. It does not offer a pleasing picture. It has little to do with what many would see as the worthwhile education of children and young adults and even less to do with a loving care for them as they seek to make sense of their world.

An extension and intensification of this policy will give an even bleaker picture. However, there is much to suggest that this is the road we are on in Britain and perhaps elsewhere. As recently as December 1998 a British government consultative green paper assumed, with a few welcome amendments, a continuation of the same school-based approach. The question is first, who wants this way of proceeding, and second, of greater importance, *why* do they want it?

2.   The second option is to make parents wholly responsible for their children's education. If, despite the measures mentioned above, the school-based system flounders and a number of schools face enforced permanent closure and others are closed frequently and for indefinite periods, it might be tempting for a government to wash its hands of the system and pass responsibility for teaching children back to the parents. Wily politicians, reading accurately the future, might forestall such a collapse and avoid recriminations by initiating an early phasing-out of schools together with the return of responsibility for children's education to parents. They might commend such a policy by claiming that:

● Some parents are already teaching their children at home successfully and enjoyably. They might publicise the large number of families in the USA and the growing number in the UK who are home-educating happily and who make no use of any school. Such families, who have had little adulation to date, might, for all the wrong reasons, find themselves held up as models!

● Some parents have given scant support to the schools in the past, and some have given none at all. Other parents complain bitterly at what has been provided, so let them, the state might argue, try to do better themselves!

● Dissatisfied parents could be given 'instruction vouchers' with which to 'buy in' teaching services from freelance, registered teachers, and 'material vouchers' for the purchase of books and equipment from approved suppliers to be used in that teaching; this would, in effect, be the privatisation of education, and be in line with the recent privatisation of several major public services in Britain and, perhaps, in other states.

3. Third, there is the option of devising a national alternative to the school-based system. A wise government will view the current education scene dispassionately and will be disturbed. It will see that serious problems currently exist, and that there may be more on the way. It will not try to pretend that all is well. If it is a responsible, caring government it will take steps, positively and seriously, to consider a range of viable and acceptable alternatives to the school-based system. Not only will this be a wise precaution, but it will have the added bonus of enabling several approaches to be evaluated calmly while there is time. Of these, one or more might prove to be as good as or better than existing provision. One approach might be so clearly superior in its motivation of children, parents and teachers, and in its range of effectiveness, that it could be given trials without delay in selected areas with volunteer families and teachers. (See also Chapter 8, *A Pilot Scheme: Five requirements* page 151).

This approach might later be offered nationally as an alternative to the school-centred organisation. Then, as is the way with these things, such a government could make a virtue of necessity and claim credit for its farsightedness, prudence, ingenuity, liberality and concern.

This last option may be the way in which reform comes about. An alarmed government, seeing the inevitable demise of traditional schooling as information technology races ahead, will bow to the inevitable and, as best it can, drag the education service into the 21st century. Sadly, if it does this, it will be reacting to events rather than leading them, and it will be acting late because exciting alternatives have been staring it in the face for a very long time.

It would be better to examine possible alternatives before the present system reaches crisis point and before emergency measures have to be initiated. But before beginning any public examination of an alternative system a government would need to answer questions likely to be raised by a concerned electorate. These questions would fall into at least twelve broad categories. They are:

1. Will the proposed scheme be viable in that it will run smoothly, be readily understood by parents and pupils, and be organised in such a way that parents and children can contribute fully to its planning and execution?
2. Will the education it offers children be richer for them emotionally, socially and intellectually than that offered now by the school-based system?
3. Will the alternative contain features which are not available already to children, parents and teachers in traditional schools?
4. Will it appeal to parents in that they will feel that they have more support in the upbringing of their children than they have at present and that this will include ample support for them in the first two years of each child's life?
5. Will the new system resolve, wholly or partly, the serious problems facing teachers in the schools, particularly problems of pupil behaviour, institutional frustration, work-induced stress and low professional esteem?
6. Will it ensure that levels of literacy and numeracy are improved?
7. Will the system benefit members of the wider community i.e. those not having a direct link with childhood education? Will members of that wider community feel that their own education can be as ongoing as they choose?
8. Will the new system be available to all parents and children who want to take part and, certainly at first, be conducted on a voluntary basis? Will traditional schools be retained for those who need or prefer them? Will this retention be long lasting?
9. Will the new approach be open to a carefully-phased introduction with all necessary information given well in advance followed by consultation meetings arranged specifically for all parents?
10. Will early education, for all children from birth to the fourteenth birthday, be removed from the party political arena?
11. Will teachers be consulted fully at all stages in the planning of the scheme, i.e. from its initial formulation to the final stages of implementation?
12. Will the teaching workforce be raised to full professional status and be of *at least* an equivalent standing to the older, self-governing callings?

3. An Outline Plan

The proposal

Early volunteers

This proposal, described in detail in Chapter 4 (pp. 36 to 130), offers a viable alternative to the 125-year-old school-based system of educating a nation's children. It makes possible a wholly personalised approach to each child's individual development. It answers questions likely to be raised by those new to the idea.

In this approach each child, from birth to his fourteenth birthday, will, with the guidance of a personal professional family tutor, be raised first within his family and then, from the approximate age of two, within his family and within his family-tutor's group of twenty personal pupils. These fourteen years will be referred to as the early-education period.

The plan proposes that the changeover from school-based education to family-based and tutor-based education is made gradually and is begun on a voluntary basis. Thus for some time the school-based system will operate alongside the new family-tutor-based approach. In circumstances where the latter presents unacceptable difficulties for child or parent or tutor or all three, or where it is for other reasons inappropriate, a modified version of the school-based system will be retained in each locality for as long as it is needed.

Schoolteachers working in the existing system who are enthusiastic about the new approach will be offered a year's full-time paid study-leave to prepare for their changed role as family personal tutors.

Working with the child's parents, each tutor will then care full-time for twenty children of roughly the same age, i.e. children within the same two-year age band. (See table page 78).

The tutor will have the same professional responsibility for the educational wellbeing of each child as a doctor in general practice has for the child's overall medical care. As with the doctor, the tutor will work with and expect co-operation from the child's parents, and, again as with the doctor, will have specialists in infant and child care available to her for consultation.

Parents will assume an ever-increasing responsibility for their child's education. The ambivalence associated with the school-based system wherein 'the teacher does this' and 'the parent does that' will be avoided. The guidance of a sympathetic professionally-trained personal tutor will be offered to parents as they perform the difficult but socially essential task of raising children. The whole of society will benefit.

Eventually, a parent who chooses to devote the whole of his or her time to educating a child – as distinct from taking paid work outside the home – will be offered comprehensive training leading to a recognised qualification in parenthood and, from that time and under a punctiliously drawn-up contract of employment, will be paid a pensionable salary appropriate to the importance of the work done and the skills required. Salary will be paid until the youngest child in the family is fourteen. Selected parents will then, if they wish, be offered a further year's salary while they train for different social work either inside or outside the education service. Fresh contracts will be drawn up for this additional paid training year and for any subsequent social work.

In the early education years parent and tutor, working closely together, will utilise varied sources of teaching material and will be able to rely especially on those services provided extensively, ubiquitously and on demand by a national central audio-visual education library (CAVEL).

The tutor, in consultation with the parent, will construct an individual study programme for each of the twenty pupils in her group. This will be drawn up having regard to: the changing needs and wishes of the child, the opinions of the parents, the range and availability of teaching materials and venues, and the tutor's professional assessment of what is best for her client. These parameters will remain in place as the programme is revised and as more teaching facilities come on stream.

The child's social development will be aided by shared activities within each tutor's personal group and through study and social contact with children in the personal groups of other tutors who practise within a tutor panel.

A tutor panel will consist of seven personal tutor groups of twenty children each, i.e. some 140 children in all. Each panel will be helped by a chairperson who will be a personal tutor elected for a two-year period by the other tutors in the panel after they have conferred with the parents of children in their groups.

The tutor panel will be linked to and registered with a very large local community resource centre whose many facilities and amenities the panel will share with eleven other tutor panels.

Each community resource centre will have a resident warden and deputy warden, both of whom will be experienced qualified tutors. They will be elected for a four-year term by the chairpersons of the panels attached to the resource centre.

There will be no fixed, formal teaching timetable or teaching venue as there is at present in the school-based system. Following family consultation, the tutor will compile her own work schedule on a week-by-week basis and select those times and study venues which are best suited to the individual child and family and to the nature of the work being undertaken.

The many possible venues will include the child's home, the tutor's study base, the community resource centre and a network of day and residential field-centres sited throughout the country. *(see Figure 9, page 98).*

The curriculum will include work in language and number, with high levels of literacy and numeracy expected of each child by age fourteen. This will be the core of the 'open' curriculum.

The 'hidden' curriculum, i.e. one whose material is taught largely incidentally, will be regarded by many as the more important. It will address the personal and social needs of the developing child. It will lay particular emphasis on the increasing amount of leisure time likely to be available to future generations as lifelong employment opportunities decrease worldwide and as the number of hours worked per week declines for many people.

In this way the personal tutor, supported by a single, influential Professional Tutors' Guild (PTG), will in all her work have in mind first the needs of the child, then those of his family, then those of the local community and, finally, the needs of the nation state.

Through the Guild, tutors will be encouraged to address the long-term needs of each generation of children for a world at peace rather than war, and where people of different nationality and race can co-exist. Throughout the whole curriculum tutors can discourage children from seeing their own nation or culture in terms of its superiority over others. The Guild will expect reciprocal measures from tutors and teachers in other countries and will stress that this is not a course which any one country can successfully negotiate on its own.

Alongside this the personal tutor, supported by the Guild, will expect the ongoing co-operation of child, family, community and nation in all her endeavours, including her aim of ensuring that her pupils have the best possible chance of becoming happy, self-confident, interesting and caring citizens. Such children, lovingly and individually catered for, will, as adults, be able in their turn to contribute much to the peaceful, selfless wellbeing of the family, community and state.

The personal tutor's role will be different from that of the classroom teacher working in today's school-based system: it will be altogether wider. The role will be less concerned with teaching directly to a set syllabus involving routine work. Technology and the immense resources of a central education library will rid the role of much of that. The professional tutor will be concerned with the personal and social development of her pupils and with aiding their families in their educational work.

In many ways the tutors' work will be more demanding than old style classteaching, but it will have immense potential for furthering professional

Figure 2. Outline of alternative education proposal.

Child: tutored by family and personal tutors from birth to 14th birth-day.

Personal tutor: guides studies of 20 children for a period of two years.

Parent: Parent is paid a salary for full-time care of child and assists personal tutor with child's education within a tutor panel.

Curriculum: The **open** curriculum will encourage love of the arts, the **hidden** respect for others and the acquiring of a set of social values.

Personal group: 20 children of similar age, and tutor, working individually or in small groups.

Local community resource centre: offers study and recreation facilities to all citizens but tutor groups have priority use of study areas.

Cavel: Central audio-visual education library produces and transmits choice of thousands of study units for parent/tutor use.

Tutor panel: consists of 7 personal groups linked to one resource centre.

Field centre: offers day and boarding accommodation to personal groups and families.

Individual study programmes: A programme compiled for each pupil for each two year period he is with one tutor and is amended as necessary: it covers a range of studies and interests.

Other venues: chosen as available by child, parent or personal tutor.

Tutor training: Tutor has honours degree and four years professional training.

Personal tutor's status: By virtue of qualifications and socially responsible work, the tutor is highly paid, highly regarded and granted full professional status.

freedom and career satisfaction. It will call for high levels of knowledge of child development and an understanding of family life. Tutors' professional training will need to reflect this and will be markedly different from the training given to teachers working at present in the school-based system. The social status and salaries accorded to tutors will reflect this. Younger tutors will find this know-ledge, experience and understanding of family life invaluable to them when they begin to raise families of their own.

If the option of paying salaries to qualified parents is disregarded, the funds needed for this alternative approach to the education of children will be no more than those now spent on the school-based system. But the money will be spent differently. Value for money will be increased. However if, as is proposed here as an option, parents who 'qualify' are paid the level of salary they would earn under contract in full time work, then more funding would be needed. Even so, much of this increased expenditure is likely to be offset by resultant savings in various areas of the social services, especially in unemployment benefit and income support. It will be money very well spent.

4. Twenty-point Project

1. Teaching children without schools

This proposal, entitled, for the sake of giving it a name, *Teaching Children Without Schools,* puts forward the possibility of educating children without recourse to a school-based system of class or subject teaching or to a curriculum constructed nationally for tens of thousands of pupils regardless of their individual needs.

It offers a wholly personal approach to education, one which suits, *per se,* each child and his parents and teachers. With the guidance of a professional personal tutor, who replaces the schoolteacher, the child is taught within the general orbit of his family and of his personal tutor's group of pupils and their families. Gradually as he grows older, his range of friends and acquaintances will be widened.

The experienced qualified teacher presently working in a school will be given the opportunity to retrain at a selected university to enable her to work as a professional personal tutor. With her pupils and their parents she will make extensive use of carefully-selected teaching materials made available to all citizens nationally and internationally by multimedia. Using these and more traditional resources, particularly literature, parents and tutor will construct individual study programmes for each of the twenty pupils in that tutor's charge. She will keep those pupils in her care for two years and come to know well each child's strengths and weaknesses and each family's attitude to, experience of, and competence in the raising of children.

With this direct and intimate approach, the love, kindness, concern and interest shown by so many teachers working in schools today, a level of care given far beyond the requirements of any formal contract and far in excess of the remuneration received, can be still further enhanced and, in future, properly rewarded.

Additionally, the long-term care given to children and parents within the family will help to restore the strength and status of the family within society, and such restoration will be fundamental to this plan. And, while the family's role will be enlarged and its responsibilities increased, it will receive caring, professional support in its difficult task for at least fourteen years.

At the same time help will be given to teachers to allow them to reallocate their personal resources. Much of the time, knowledge, nervous energy, materials and professional skills presently used uneconomically by teachers in meeting the demands of school organisation, local and central government bureaucracy, anxious parents and dissatisfied pupils, can be redirected to meeting the individual requirements of children. Increasing work satisfaction and rapidly declining school-generated frustration will bring relief to thousands of teachers. Some, now on the point of leaving their jobs, may be persuaded to stay and retrain for something better within the new system. Parents currently facing the sacrifices called for by fee-paying in the private school option will be able to give the new education service their support. They will save money and, in some cases, salve happily their social consciences.

2. The children

While this plan helps children, parents, the state and teachers, and while all of these are important, it is the first group, the children, who are the principal clients and thus the most important. Their parents are the second group of beneficiaries. Each state's influence, as in many areas of national life, will steadily decline even though, through its taxation system, it will be paying tutors and providing the other material resources necessary for the operation of the education service. Eventually, however, the benefits of teaching-without-schools will spread to all the four parties involved: children, parents, teachers and state.

The plan will improve pupils' wellbeing in at least three ways. It will:

● Have regard and concern for them as individuals who have rights, interests and expectations of their own with, as they grow older, opportunities to take on corresponding responsibilities.
● Offer them a readily-available, known, trusted, caring and skilled adult to whom, in addition to their parents and other family members, they can turn for the comfort, consolation, counselling, encouragement and impartial advice they need so often.
● Assure them that they are increasingly involved in the construction of their personal study plan and that their views, preferences and difficulties will be listened to sympathetically throughout its implementation. They will know that what they think really does matter.

This personal involvement in an individually-designed plan will be present from an early stage and will increase as the child grows older. It will be quite considerable by ages eight to nine. In the final two years of early education, at ages twelve and thirteen, the child will be encouraged to build his own pro-gramme, with his tutor, and then to seek parental and tutorial support in seeing it through *(see section 18 Individual study programmes, pages 113 to 118, and Figure 12 on page 116).*

Teaching a child in this way instead of, for instance, as one unit in a class of 35 in a school of 700, will reduce the likelihood of labelling, boredom, frustration, antagonism or sheer indifference. It will avoid the possible build-up of a resentful, anti-teacher, anti-school attitude: there will be no teachers and no schools for young people to resent.

Any experienced schoolteacher will concur that three or four children taught as a small group, or individually, can be quite different in attitude and behaviour from when those same children are taught in a class of thirty or forty. Singly they are usually amenable, attentive, industrious and co-operative and are better able to establish sound working relationships with their teachers.

Wealthy families who employ trained nannies and then highly-qualified private tutors for their children's early education know both what they are paying for and why they are paying for it. So do those upper-middle-class parents of more modest means who value the small classes or study groups found in most fee-paying private schools. Both require the individual needs of their children to be given the ongoing personal attention of caring, well-educated adults: that is what the extra money buys.

If there are benefits to be derived from teaching some favoured children individually and in small groups, methods can be designed today to pass on such benefits to all children. From that development the whole of society will gain. But at the moment, in most industrialised countries, the position is that many of those in least need tend to get personal and privileged attention, while those in greatest need of help and support are placed in large classes to follow, for fixed school hours, with relatively poor resources, a standardised, impersonal curriculum. This is a worldwide problem which affects, or will affect, all countries.

From it arise situations where children from desperately deprived areas can be taught, in large groups, about the Charge of the Light Brigade in the Crimean War, or the value of X if Y equals 4 and Z equals something else, or the source of the Nile, or the life cycle of the common amoeba.

In that class may be children for whom such topics have no possible relevance. Peter, whose father has just lost another job; Alan, whose mother is pregnant for the seventh time; Julia, whose brother is unemployed and on probation; Jack, whose hated 'uncle' has moved into his house permanently; Sarah, whose alcoholic neighbours have threatened her dog; Tina, whose family have been told to quit their house; Arthur, whose twin brothers have been diagnosed as epileptic; Winston, who is racially taunted in the streets; Tom, who has been caught shoplifting, and Jean who has been abused for years by an older cousin.

At the other end of the socio-economic scale, on the far side of town in a costly, tree-surrounded school with private lake and swimming pool, are Clive, Sheila, Douglas and Stephanie.

Clive has his own attractive study-bedroom with much new electronic equipment and parents who are rarely at home to talk to him. Sheila lives in a fine detached house with an acre of garden and has an extensive wardrobe and parents whose bitter rows echo through the house until the early hours. Douglas, an only child, has parents who are such keen golfers that they have little interest in anything else, so that despite holidays in exotically-golf-coursed countries, Douglas is bored and depressed. Stephanie, who lives with a wealthy grandmother following the death of her parents years before, finds making friends difficult and has been experimenting with 'soft' drugs as yet unnoticed by grandparent or the teachers in this 'high-fee' school.

Even in schools which are outwardly so different, what is being taught frequently has little bearing on the personal needs of the pupils attending. The size and subsequent organisation of the schools and the priorities enforced by a national curriculum or examination board's syllabus make it difficult for teachers to identify quickly and fully the personal problems and real needs of their pupils. Even if such recognition was immediately possible, the workload, class-control demands and lack of direct, ongoing communication with parents would make it well-nigh impossible for these teachers to make adequate impact on dangerous situations and great unhappiness. Such pupils and, to a lesser extent their teachers, are victims of an often outdated, impersonal and now unnecessary school-based system.

3. The parents

There is much in modern western society which gives cause for concern about the weakening of family ties: the effectiveness of control of children by parents, by schools and by other authorities, and the confidence of adults generally to cope with the apparently anti-social behaviour of some young children and adolescents.

A major aim of this alternative education plan will be to help parents and other family members assume increased responsibility for their children's education and lifestyle and, at the same time, gain greater pleasure and satisfaction from the years they spend on the upbringing of their children.

'Education' will be interpreted broadly. It will be seen as the assimilation of all that is good in the nation's culture. This selection will include compassion, helpfulness, industriousness, personal responsiblllty, liuuesly and a love for the arts, all of which have made possible mankind's progression – however fitful and at times unsure – from distant savage to reasonably acceptable civilised being. Put another way, education, as it is seen in a teaching-without-schools context, will be instrumental in the further sophistication of humankind.

'Education' then will not be restricted to those activities which, traditionally, have been undertaken in schools or colleges. It will include consideration of much that is learned inside and outside the home. There will be ongoing discussion of the consequences of differing social behaviour in the family, amongst peers, and in the wider community and of the need, for the common good, of unselfish living.

At a national level this movement away from the school and back to the family – with the responsibility for young people's welfare shared between home and personal tutors – will be gradual and extend over several generations. Parents' opportunities to be the master-builders of their children's behaviour patterns will increase as that of school, church, peer group and the entertainment media decline. There will be great satisfaction in this work for parents as help is offered and as their skills and understanding grow. At the same time the responsibilities of parents will increase. Acceptance of these responsibilities at times when things go wrong, as well as when they are successful, will be part of the social contract.

If this plan is introduced fully, there will, by the year 2099, be only a tiny minority of variously-incapacitated parents who will not be responsible, with professional help, for the whole of their children's upbringing and behaviour until those children reach the legal age of majority which is currently, in Britain, eighteen.

This will include the undertaking by parents of full-time supervision of their child's education. They will not be working alone here, but will have the support and, where necessary the guidance, of tutors. There will be the provision, nationally and locally, of tested and graded educational material. The work of all parents will be as stimulating, enjoyable and rewarding as it is already for those parents who appreciate fully the value of the work they undertake with their children and who have all the resources necessary for its successful completion.

Parents who opt for this alternative approach to their children's education will attend lectures, seminars and tutorials at community resource centres or at a local university, or both. These sessions will be generously augmented by programmes and lessons from the Central Audio-Visual Education Library (CAVEL) transmitted to their homes.

Parents, rightly, will become highly knowledgeable in all aspects of child development. The 'hit and miss', 'hope for the best', 'do what Mum did' attitudes of the past – when anyone could attempt to raise a child no matter how sparse his or her knowledge of children – or how weak the enthusiasm – will be gone. The exceptionally responsible task of raising children will be recognised, appreciated and rewarded by an indebted society. While this will be a remarkable departure from past practice, it is one that a Western developed society can now afford and one which will be an investment from which all citizens will benefit.

A key factor in the education available to parents will be a frank recognition of how difficult and sensitive relationships within a family can be, and how these change as relationships mature and as children grow older and seek increasing levels of independence. The pressure from the media, peer groups and role models on children to seek a pseudo-independence at an ever-earlier age adds to a parent's problems: it calls out for skilled help from a personal tutor and tutor panel. These demands from children often coincide with stressful times in the parents' marriage, career or financial situation and this adds to the need for expert outside help. Fortunately, although in an official sense the help given by tutors will come from *outside* the family, by the time a child is ten or eleven the trusting and intimate relationship that has developed between the tutorial group panel and the family will, for all intents and purposes, be an *internal* one.

The parent will have the opportunity, with all necessary professional assistance, to plan the child's study programme from before its birth until its fourteenth birthday. In that way the plan will reflect the child's aptitudes and interests and also the parent's own carefully considered, realistically-viewed and socially-responsible aspirations for the child. These factors are clearly interlinked, and a perceptive tutor will need patience, foresight and the power of persuasion to ensure that one aspect is not dominated by any other. A significant part of each tutor's training will address these issues and fully-qualified status will not be awarded by the PTG until such time as the probationary tutor can demonstrate the necessary understanding and skill.

An important part of parental education will be the objective discussion of desirable family size as social changes take place if and when the subject is raised by the parents. This might be incidental in the course of other work, or after a formal talk or film. In considering individual family size, factors to be borne in mind will include personal preferences, family budget, home space, parental and other family and work commitments, and the level of interest a parent has in the newly-appreciated work of child-rearing. At a national and international level the whole complex question of population management and finite global resources will need to be considered as a crucial and ongoing matter.

But this vital policy of worldwide population control stands little chance of succeeding unless 'ordinary' people understand, through their education, the nature of world population problems and the cultural difficulties that stand in the way of control. This reappraisal of attitudes will require the understanding and help of tutors and of parents and young people, too. The parents' role, as well as the tutors', will change, and the objectives they seek will change with them.

What parents are being asked to do in the whole delicate area of family care is to undertake difficult, expensive-to-fund duties from which, ultimately, the whole of society will gain. The movement away from nine years of school-based early education (5-14 years), to professionally assisted home-based early education lasting fourteen years (0-14 years), will be placing considerable extra demands on parents. In terms of the changes made in the last 100 years, the movement will be revolutionary and not all families will be prepared or able to participate. But where parents accept such a task – one having obligations as well as rewards – society should be willing to pay generously for its introduction.

Where parents agree to undertake this work as a full-time, skilled and carefully-executed occupation, such parenting will be treated as a high-status calling. It will be one which enjoys all the rights, support and protection of any other work. Apart from the profession of tutoring, no other occupation will have greater prestige. This, too, will be revolutionary, and the internalising or absorbing of such ideas in any society will take several decades – or one, if not two, generations.

People's attitudes worldwide will need to change in many ways. Significant will be the equal treatment – financially, legally and socially – of the roles of father and mother. Where cultural differences in the treatment of boys and girls still exist, either socially or educationally, these will need to be discouraged.

But another difficult change to engineer will be that of accepting the need to spend a far greater proportion of gross national product on the new teaching-without-schools programme. A steady, clever and effective policy of enlightenment will be needed. To take two instances of how fundamental such attitude changes will need to be, nations will have to adjust to the idea of paying tutors more than they now pay the average general medical practitioner, and to paying a parent engaged in the full-time education of his or her children a salary equal to that of any other experienced, qualified, skilled worker.

Eventually society will need to agree to further funds being allocated to help families adapt and to furnish accommodation for educational needs, and in providing for the tutoring needs of children in the two youngest age groups [birth to four years] i.e. age groups not fully catered for in existing educational expenditure.

While there is little to disagree with in the notion that parents be more involved with their children's education, the proposal that either the mother or the father be paid a full salary for full-time work will be more contentious.

The proposal is that the parent or guardian who chooses to work full-time in the home co-operating with the personal tutor in the education of his or her child will receive a salary from the state paid for through general taxation. The salary will be on a set scale. It will be the same no matter how many of his or her children the parent is helping to educate, although the home-based education *expenses* allowed will be greater for two or more children. The point on the parental salary scale at which the parent is first placed will depend on the qualifications held and the experience already gained in parenting.

If, for example, the salary is set at £15,000 in Britain, or US$ 25,000, a parent with basic training and no experience will begin at 60% of that amount. One who successfully completes a six-month part-time course will begin at 70%, or for a one-year full-time course 80%. One who gains a university degree in child care, education and parenthood will receive 95%. Annual increments will be added for satisfactory experience and study to a maximum of fourteen years. Thus a graduate with full incremental experience will earn about £25,000 or US $42,000 on today's (1999) scale and exchange rate. Such a graduate parent, once interviewed and approved, will then be offered further truncated training with a view to becoming a fully-qualified personal professional tutor. Others will be offered a further year's salary if they train full-time for alternative work after all their children have passed the age of fourteen and moved on to middle education college.

The sums needed for this provision will be large and have not been fully allowed for in the initial funding of the trial or pilot schemes for this plan. But the idea should not be dismissed out of hand simply because of the costs involved.

As many nations are discovering, inadequate provision for early childhood education can prove to be expensive later on in terms of little learning, poor motivation, indifferent attitudes, juvenile delinquency, stressed parents and disillusioned teachers. There is too little appreciation of the strain placed on a parent and often on an infant or early grade schoolteacher in caring for very young children. In either case the work can be lonely and repetitive, and either poorly paid in the case of teachers, or not at all in the case of parents. Under this proposal, child-raising will become for a parent a valued, salaried practice, and for the teacher an altogether more rewarding occupation.

Even so, 'return on investment' will not be immediately measurable as it is when money is put into the manufacturing or service industries. Because of this there will be scepticism, but there will also be direct savings in terms of unemployment pay and social benefit costs as many jobs released by newly-salaried parents are taken up by other workers. There will be growing savings from a reduction in vandalism and other crime and from the probationary surveillance of many young people. A large number of parents currently under stress at having to hold down a job and care for their children will be relieved of this strain, be in better health themselves, and so make fewer demands on the health services. All this will reduce the total financial costs of the new non-school-based approach to childhood education.

But the great gains will be those made in terms of family happiness. This cannot be costed directly. Nor can the increased work-satisfaction of teachers, nor, put in mercenary terms, can the value given by them in their jobs. Both will be reflected in an enhanced quality of life for millions of people.

Of far greater importance eventually will be the recognition that preparing children for living in one global society and making good provision for future generations is a vital matter. It is the equal, on any assessment, of all other work, and must be seen as such. The advantages to each state and to a world society of more richly-reared children within knowledgeable family circles will be beyond any accountant's ability to measure.

Parents already, in the school-based system, need respite care. Opportunities for respite currently offered by child hours spent at school are insufficient, especially if there are younger children not yet at school or if both parents need to work outside the home to raise income levels. Under the new plan, which will make far greater demands on parents, respite care will need to be regular, substantial and mandatory. Funding will be required not only to give parents a break but to enable them to give of their best when working with their children and their children's tutors. The whole concept of parenthood will be revolutionised. From being an unpaid, lowly-regarded job for which no preparation is thought to be needed and for which little is available, it will become a highly-regarded, fully-trained, generously-paid profession which is socially rewarding and locally, nationally and internationally supported.

In the provision of respite care, social facilities will be provided for parents enabling them to relax and enjoy the company and reassurance of other adults. Much of this provision will be at local community resource centres (see p. 86) and will be available throughout the day. Eventually such centres will offer twenty-four hour opening. Field centres (page 92) will also be used.

Financial support for parents will not be limited to a salary and home-education expenses. The salary will attract all national insurance benefits and contributions. It will be inflation-linked and fully pensionable in terms of the years of service given.

However, it is likely that some parents will remain unconvinced and will choose not to participate. They will conclude that their children will be better served by the existing school-based system. Their decision will be one that has been reached after much discussion, thought and calculation, and one which will be respected.

Other groups of parents will be indifferent to, or opposed to, the new proposals for teaching-children-without-schools: some of those will be uncooperative in any system and some will be unwilling to lose the important child-minding function of the traditional school – a function they have taken for granted for many years.

Parental indifference might arise from a general inability or unwillingness to see that any benefits can arise for them or for any of their children from any system of education whether it be old and reactionary or new and revolutionary or anything that falls between. They see all schooling as a serving of time as in a conscripted army or in a prison: you get through it, leave it, and then resume real life. Such indifference will mean they will not bother to enrol their children with a tutor group or enrol themselves with classes alongside other parents who are studying child development and upbringing.

Others might be opposed to the new scheme because they do not see it meeting their needs. Opposition may be residual: they gained nothing from their schools, they disliked school, related poorly to teachers and failed in examinations, as did their own parents and grandparents. Today they do not trust teachers: teachers are part of 'them' and 'them' is the establishment. No matter how any new education system is packaged and presented they will see tutors as teachers. They will see the new system as a mere revamping of the old except that it will seem to have the additional insult of intruding into their private family lives. But there may be a change of mind when it is realised that families in the new system are gaining many benefits and when many of the initially resistant parents begin to seek similar benefits for their own children.

Opposition of a different kind might come from those parents who see themselves as overall losers under the alternative approach. These will be people who depend on the set school day, week and term for their own highly-paid employment, relaxation, hobbies, social contacts and family holidays. Further opposition might come from those who feel they profited greatly from their own schooling and who are, therefore, happy to see their own children offered the same opportunities under the same system. They are content with things as they are. So, for one reason or another, many parents may not wish to be involved initially in any new approach to education no matter how carefully it has been thought out, whoever introduces it, or however beneficial it might be to them in the long term.

In the light of these factors, and no doubt others, the school-based system will need to operate alongside the new system for an indefinite period. People must know, from the start, that this is going to happen. There can be no compulsion for anyone to take part in the new system, and compulsion will not be sought by practitioners in the personal tutor organisation. Compulsion will be seen as wholly incompatible with education; the first negates the second. Particularly with early proponents of the new system, compulsion will be anathema and so rejected.

It will be pointed out that the old nineteenth century schooling of children gained little if anything from the compulsory attendance of the unwilling, and there is a strong case now for forced attendance being abolished in the school-based system: like oil and water, compulsion and education do not mix. There will be no case at all for compulsion in the new system: it would be a denial of all that the system stands for. Those indifferent to or opposed to the new arrangement must be under no obligation to transfer to it from the schools. The new 21st century system needs to be built not on the compulsory attendance principle inherited by schools from the laws of the 1870s and 1880s, but on a real desire to participate on the part of every parent and later, as they grow older, of every pupil.

Paid employment, of any kind, of children who are not currently undertaking education in either system will need to be strictly prohibited with legislation in place to ensure this. There will be no question of any return to the 19th century exploitation of child labour by unscrupulous employers, acquiescent parents or an indifferent society.

There will be some exceptions to the principle that only eager parents and children will participate in the new approach. Examples might be those parents who, while they have doubts about some aspects of teaching-children-without-schools, will feel that the proposal offers an escape from a school-based system in which they have no confidence at all. Or there may be those who, because they had no faith in the prospects offered to their children by traditional state schools in their district, made use reluctantly of private schools. This use might have been at variance with their conscience, at the expense of their bank balance, and at the risk of some social isolation. In the new approach such parents might see some of their problems resolved and so might opt for enrolment in the new system.

But at present there can be no doubt that too many aspects of a child's upbringing are left to chance. There is no reliable evidence of exactly how many children suffer in families where there is little understanding of the needs of children and where there is even less knowledge of how those needs might be met. Parental skills are still difficult to obtain even though there has been an increase in the number of classes on offer in different areas. If parents themselves have had a deprived upbringing and have had no opportunity to observe other families' different lifestyles, they are likely to regard their own practices as the norm. If, in addition, there is a shortage of money and living space, and no job security, then too much is being asked of too many parents. Their children, in no way responsible for this unsatisfactory situation, will, largely unknown to the rest of society, be the ones to suffer most. They are the really vulnerable ones and are the ones who most need help. Yet, within this all-too-familiar scenario, teachers, working in some of the least attractive neighbourhoods, often in the least attractive buildings, are called upon to teach children from diverse backgrounds in classes of thirty or more almost as if nothing had happened to those children before they reached compulsory school attendance age.

Any experienced teacher of young children will agree that when children appear at school for their first day around the age of five years – six in the USA – some are able to read and write, draw and paint, cut and stick, calculate, converse, listen attentively, make up their own stories, relate them to others and add thoughtful comments at the same time. Some will be looking forward to school having been prepared positively for it by highly-literate, enthusiastic parents who still value their own schooldays. The children enjoy what is done and relate well with children of a similar social background and with their teachers. They accept the behaviour code necessary for the safe running of the classroom and school. They want to do well. All these factors – social class, intelligence, family support, neighbourhood, peer group values, motivation, confidence and expectations, usually ensure they do very well indeed: they make success at school a fairly safe bet and such children are likely to benefit from whatever education the school can offer. Cynics might add that these children will do well *despite* the school! As educational sociologists will indicate, these fortunate children have a high level of educability.

The same teacher will tell you of other children who have few or none of these advantages. They will appear at the school gates unprepared in any way for the day ahead. Their educability level will be as low as the first group's is high. Even before these two groups of children are assembled on their first morning and before their teacher has spent her first hours with them, the range of differences will be seen to be immense. From then on, with few exceptions, that range of differences will grow with every month that passes.

It is cruel, in these circumstances, to talk of 'equality of opportunity' as if it can be engineered by schools or produced from a hat by slick politicians. It is nonsense. It cannot, and no good can be served by pretending otherwise.

Sometimes schools, by their very size, structure and locality can only, over time, exacerbate the range of differences. Politicians and educational administrators, who, by continuing to think of education only in terms of what schools can do, often make things worse.

This concept of 'educability' is, perhaps, the most helpful to be provided by educational sociologists for the past fifty years. It gives a starting-point for change and, with it, hope for rectification. It upholds the notion that schools are not necessarily the most appropriate vehicles for transforming the lifestyles and life opportunities of many disadvantaged children. Nor need they be best for pupils from economically-favoured and well-educated families. Educability tells us how complex is the interaction between the many different factors which advance or retard a child's learning. School is but one factor and it may now, for many children, be one with which we can dispense.

All the factors which combine so intricately to shape a child's future must be addressed, and this must be done within the broad sociological context of the family and not in the narrow, curriculum-restricted climate of the schools. Parents, given consistent help, have to be involved in education and upbringing from their child's conception, and must continue to be involved at least throughout his fourteen early-education years.

Children from families in low socio-economic groups, children from exceptionally favoured backgrounds and all those of very high or very low intelligence might be ill-served by the inevitable degree of uniformity found in many schools.

While it is true that a child of low educability will suffer from lack of adequate preparation, inability to comprehend much of the language used, insufficient powers of concentration, or ineptness at abiding by a fixed routine, some of the most able children from any background may become bored, apathetic, rebellious and a distraction to others if their schools cannot provide for their equally special need for different, rapidly-accelerating and demanding study programmes. Children of high intelligence and those with special talents can become deprived children if their needs are not recognised early and then catered for adequately over the long term.

When children have an unusually high or unusually low level of educability there is an ever-present danger that schools, with their need to relate to and keep control of hundreds of 'average' children while at the same time delivering a nationally-imposed curriculum and the associated testing, will, despite the best of intentions, be unable to provide fully for those children's special needs.

It is not the fault of the teachers nor, in most cases, the parents. It is the result of all the parties responsible for popular childhood education continuing to work almost entirely within the parameters of an old-fashioned school-based institution. This long-protected institution appears to be doing damage by delaying or discouraging experimentation with the range of alternatives currently available to children, parents and teachers.

While the existing school system will not *prohibit* new approaches as such, as has been shown by those parents who already opt for and use an alternative to the school for their children, the institution's very presence, embedded deeply in Western culture, is a discouragement to experimentation. So strong is the 'belief' in the school that even those parents and teachers who would be willing to put to the test possible alternatives are inhibited from doing so. They look at the century-long life of the school and the apparent readiness of millions of parents to use its facilities for their children, and they begin to think to themselves:

"It must be me. I must be the one who is wrong – the one out of step. Perhaps all that is remiss of the school is my attitude to it. I must try again and give it another chance..."

And so another doubter buries her doubts and begins to think – or hope – that if the school undergoes another series of minor adjustments it will, eventually, meet society's needs. All one can say is that such success is a long time coming.

The entrenched notion that schooling *is* education and vice versa can make people blind to what else might be done. From their televisions, radios and newspapers people know that not all is well with the schools and that some change is indicated. But people are led to believe that such change can be devised only within the existing system. Little, if any, publicity is given to those feasible alternatives already to hand.

Parents have to be convinced that they must be brought fully into the educative process, assured that they can succeed, and attracted into partnership with understanding personal tutors working in an alternative, up to date system.

4. The nation state

As the centuries pass, nations themselves will become convenient administrative centres in a global society. But, until that happens, existing nations will slowly change to the teaching-without-schools system and will play a decreasing role in the education of children. While it is likely that one state, probably the UK or the USA, will lead in offering this alternative, others will need to follow quickly because a movement away from nationalistic teaching will, as in other fields, be difficult for any one country to sustain if there is no evidence of willing and wholesale reciprocal actions by the others.

As the curriculum, like the increasingly global society, becomes increasingly "denationalised", its individualisation will enable parent and tutor to decide what needs to be taught to whom, and when and where and how.

But the state will not lose by this retirement from the educational scene. Over the ensuing years it will gain happier, more interesting and more responsible citizens who will wonder at the 20th century's approval and enforcement of a standardised national curriculum, centrally imposed and tested, regardless of children's individual needs. They will marvel, for instance, that in the last decades of the century successive governments were offering more of the same: a continuation of school inspection policies, frequent and rigorous assessment of children and teachers, and performance-related pay. This unhappy lack of imagination and warm, human feeling in a service which should be brimful of both was deeply disturbing to many thoughtful observers..

It takes little prescience to see that as technology progresses and increasingly undertakes work once done routinely by men and women, future citizens will need a range of interests beyond paid employment. For many vulnerable people permanent, lifelong employment will not be available. Those politicians who claim otherwise are holding out unrealistic promises to susceptible voters.

If viewed negatively, as wholly unwelcome, the reactions to unemployment of the millions affected by it will be boredom, disillusionment, shame and despair, to be followed, possibly, by antagonism towards authority. Not only are the dangers painfully obvious, but they are already here in Britain just as they are in many de-industrialising countries.

Such dangers can be avoided in part if each state is honest in recognising future trends and does not raise unfounded hopes that one day all citizens will return to full employment. The nation state must ensure that individuals are introduced to many worthwhile pursuits which will offer a lifetime of interest and enjoyment and lead, perhaps, to alternative employment opportunities at some time in the future. The Protestant, capitalist work ethic will come to be seen as a phenomenon of a different era and will be allowed to wither away. People will be encouraged, for the first time, to enjoy their lives free of the dominance of work: work which for many was dangerous, unhealthy, demeaning, tedious, uncertain and ill-paid.

It will be this freedom from full-time work that will enable many parents, with the assistance of professional personal tutors, to devote the time necessary to educate their young children. From this the whole state will benefit. Indeed the whole world would gain if, as a matter of course, some of this work with older children could be done abroad. It would be an important step towards the internationalisation of society. There would be reductions in tensions and less likelihood of misunderstandings, hostility and war. So what will be needed from the nation state throughout the 21st century will be imagination in its educational thinking and a readiness to innovate.

5. The funds needed

Once the new system of teaching-children-without-schools is operational, the annual funding required will be similar to that now allocated to the school-based system.

The plan will be operated initially on a voluntary basis with sufficient participants enrolled to make viable the operation of one local community resource centre. This centre will be obtained by the allocation to the scheme of one underused secondary school. An about-to-be-closed village primary school in another part of the same county will become a field centre.

The normal per-capita allowances for 1,400 school-based pupils will be adequate for the 1,400 children (aged from birth to fourteen) who will be involved in the pilot scheme. It will pay the ongoing costs of salaries, buildings, books and equipment. Although not an essential factor, it is likely that those parents volunteering will be enthusiastic about the scheme and anxious for it to succeed and will, as many parents already do with schools, contribute additional time and money to the exciting trial project of which they will be part.

Once the plan is put into nationwide operation the costs will be modest. They will involve the provision of a national central audio-visual education library (CAVEL), large local community resource centres, field centres, child-parent-tutor study facilities and transport.

Capital costs will be met from the sale of unwanted schools and their land. Many of these redundant properties will, because of their prime sitings, command high prices. Even so, in the early years, some large secondary schools will need to be retained for use as resource centres, and others for continuing use as schools to cater for those families who do not wish to be involved immediately in the new approach.

Ongoing costs will be met from and be equivalent to the funds currently raised to support the school-based system.

Two areas not directly covered by current costs will be:

(i) provision for the children aged from birth to four years who are not at present in full-time education, and
(ii) provision of salaries to 'qualified' parents in lieu of earnings attainable by them in other work.

Some of the extra money needed for the youngest children will come from savings in current nursery school and part-time infant school expenditure and other costs, and from savings made from the expensive upkeep of thousands of school buildings.

Some of the costs of providing full-time parents with salaries will come from savings on income support and other social services and from cuts made possible in unemployment and other benefits as more jobs are released by full-time parents: these savings could be substantial and the social value to the country of the return to work of millions will be inestimable in terms of mere pounds or dollars.

The pilot scheme and the plan's later, wide adoption could go ahead without either or both of these additional costs. Initially the youngest children might be excluded and parental salaries not paid. This would enable the plan, as far as it goes, to be judged on present costs. But it would be incomplete and, in view of the sums saved, undesirable.

It is likely, however, that when it is seen that the new system is giving good value for money in a variety of ways, each nation will be willing to increase the percentage of gross national product allocated to education, and that many more parents and others will do as some do now and contribute voluntarily their time, skills and cash.

6. The teachers and tutors

The new education system will change the teacher's role. By freeing teachers of the physical constraints of the school's buildings and the restrictions on innovation inevitable in an institutionalised hierarchical structure, teachers, or tutors, will become creative decision-makers in their own right. They will, as practitioners responsible for their decisions and actions, join the ranks of the established professions. They will, in the course of their work, decide on and do whatever is best for their clients.

Given the importance of the teachers' task, professional status should have been accorded to teachers a century ago, but a sad combination of factors prevented this from happening and, unfortunately, many of these factors remain in place today.

There is little point now in trying to apportion blame for these shortcomings, and teachers themselves are far from blameless. There has been their ongoing inability or unwillingness to act as one body with one voice. They have permitted – even encouraged – splits to develop within the teaching workforce which employers at both national and local levels have been able to use effectively to play off teaching factions one against another. This has weakened teachers as a group and has probably had some indeterminate part to play in keeping salaries and pensions low. It has also made the public as a whole sceptical of teachers' claims for higher status when teachers themselves appear to spend so much time, money and effort in squabbling and in-fighting.

In the long run, of course, this has been detrimental to all parties, including the nation state. It has resulted in a dissatisfaction within the profession that can do no good to that very section of society that state education should be aiming to serve: middle and working-class children and their parents.

No long-term view has been taken by governments of the effects likely on the morale of teachers brought on by fifty years of strife both within the teaching force and between it and its local and national employers. In the UK matters have been allowed to stumble on from one acrimonious pay settlement to the next, with teachers' representatives bickering amongst themselves about who gets most of an inadequate overall sum, or about which union best serves teachers' interests.

As it seems unlikely that teachers will put their own house in order, the state would do itself and everyone else much good if it established a *fully self-regulating* General Teaching Council (GTC) on the same lines as, *and wholly on a par with*, the British Medical Association (BMA), and encouraged vigorously and resolutely a wholesome feeling of professionalism among teachers. The state might have to pay more as salaries were raised and conditions improved, but it would be money spent for the general good of the state's children, parents, teachers and other citizens. The timing would be highly beneficial if this expenditure by the state coincided with the advent of teaching-without-schools and the removal of the institutionalised teaching hierarchy.

Thus, as far as this book is concerned, the most important factor in the long-running saga of whether schoolteaching is a profession or not is the existence of the school itself. Much has had to be sacrificed by teachers, perhaps unwittingly, in order to allow the institution to be maintained and to continue largely unchallenged from one century to another.

Under this plan for educating the future, most children up to the age of fourteen will be taught without recourse to schools, and so a major factor in the holding back of teachers' professional aspirations will be removed at a stroke. This removal will have several dramatic and immediate effects.

For instance, for the last 125 years it has been argued, or assumed, that the school as we know it has needed a headteacher: someone who is paid substantially more than the classroom teacher, someone who leads the rest of 'her' teaching staff and who is responsible to governors and others for all that happens in 'her' school. This widely held concept of headteachership has undermined the status of the other teachers in the school, both in their estimation of themselves and in the estimation of others outside the school. It implies that teachers need to be 'led', that they cannot be trusted to work without a 'boss', that they cannot accept responsibility for their own actions or manage their own work schedule. Further, in too many cases, that they cannot be allowed to have direct access to their pupils' parents: there has to be present an intermediary of superior status.

Teachers other than the headteacher are often referred to as 'assistant teachers'. Not only is this a derogatory title, but often it is laughable, for it implies that the headteacher teaches and the assistant assists her. Frequently the school-generated and externally-imposed bureaucracy is so great that the headteacher teaches far less than those who are supposed to be 'assisting' and the title becomes a misnomer.

In effect it is often the assistant who does the teaching while the headteacher arranges the organisation of the school. The headteacher decides who is to teach which children, when, where and for how long. She also determines how the school's other resources are to be used, what administrative arrangements are to be made and who on the staff is to be 'promoted' to a higher level in a sometimes ludicrous, unnecessary and insulting pecking order.

Inevitably this removes from the assistant teacher much of the decision-making freedom, responsibility and status she needs if she is to rank as an independent professional person. She does not choose her clients, she is limited in what she can teach and constrained in her practice by the logistics enforced by the school structure in which she works. She does not have direct, ongoing dealings with parents and thus knows little about half her client base. She is subject to the rulings of those who, while of lower rank than her headteacher, are a step or two above her own: there may be one or more deputy heads, heads of years or departments, heads of curriculum or pastoral care, and heads responsible for this and that and the other. Profession it is not.

There may be times when the assistant teacher disagrees profoundly with some or most of the decisions made on teaching policy. She will be unhappy with the ways in which such policies are subsequently implemented and the way in which they affect adversely her work. But, apart from resigning her post, there is little she can do but work to a ruling with which she has little sympathy or enthusiasm. This is wrong.

Matters can be worse when she sees that the method of appointment of those above her in the hierarchy can be arbitrary, haphazard, fortuitous or based on the personal preference of whoever is doing the appointing on the day.

It is difficult to measure the level of frustration aroused by being able to see a different and better way of practising her calling and then being denied the opportunity to do so by someone less competent, intelligent, imaginative, questioning or determined than herself.

The psychological damage being done may be invisible to all but the most perceptive, but it is there and it does the mental health of that teacher – and perhaps others on the staff – no good at all. In Britain, certainly, no sensitive, idealistic, creative person who is brimming over with ideas would ever be advised to enter teaching as it stands today. Nor would anyone whose natural inclination it is "never to stop questioning" what is going on. And that is everyone's loss: including the government's.

But the damage is greater than that. Such a teacher, who has to go on working in schools run habitually in that way, is compromising her own integrity. She is placed in a false position because, in front of thirty or more children, she has to smile and pretend that everything in the playground is lovely when, in fact, it is not. At times it must be asking the impossible.

Some may claim that teachers lack the initiative to work on their own or to make their own decisions. Teachers, they say, need to be 'led' by headteachers and both need to be 'kept in line' by teams of wandering inspectors. This seems doubtful to say the least, and, even if it does apply to a small proportion of teachers and headteachers, that is no justification for imposing on all the others a level of control needed only by a tiny minority. That minority should be directed to less responsible work elsewhere with the remaining large majority freed to practise professionally with appropriate remuneration. If the assertion of inadequacy is true of more than a small minority then questions need to be asked as to why teaching as an occupation – perhaps the most important occupation – is unable to recruit and retain practitioners of sufficiently high calibre to confirm teaching as a fully-fledged profession. And the questions need to be answered honestly and fully.

But the calibre of the teaching force – whatever it is – cannot be separated from the school-based system in which it tries to work. It is the school which has given rise to the occupational structure of teaching as it is today and to the lack of appeal it has as a career. It is the institution of school, and what it is doing, which needs to be examined first. It is difficult to see how the structure of teaching can be radically changed and teachers given their independence while the school-based system remains as it is.

But once the school goes, tremendous opportunities are opened up for teachers. Many things will change as an alternative system is introduced. But the change is unlikely to be painless: teachers will not be set for an easy transition.

The calibre of candidates offering themselves for the tutoring profession will need to be high. The selection procedure will need to be long and rigorous and certainly as searching as that for army officers, general medical practitioners or senior civil servants. The training which follows will need to be tough and comprehensive. Throughout the training process, academically weak or temperamentally unsuitable students will be required to withdraw. Theoretical and practical examinations will be demanding. The period of probationary service following initial qualification will be long and meaningful, and one which must be satisfactorily completed before full membership of the tutors' professional association, the PTG, is awarded and its licence to practise accorded.

Once full professional status has been acquired – both by the individual and by the whole tutoring body – strict rules and self-regulation will apply to personal tutors as they do to other professionals.

The tutor will be proud of the work she does and she will recognise its value. She will not denigrate her work or make apologies for it; "I'm only a teacher – I didn't really want to teach but there was nothing else going at the time". Nor will she pay heed to cheap remarks of the kind that refer to a teacher as 'a man among boys, a boy among men', or who claim that 'those who can, do; those who can't, teach!'

She will accept responsibility for the decisions she makes and the work which follows; there will be no headteacher to run to, no head of department to blame, no national curriculum to ease selection of material. She will arrange her own schedule, work very long hours, often be 'on call' at unusual times and frequently assist parents as well as pupils.

She will be loyal to her colleagues but will not cover up incompetence or unprofessional behaviour. She will update her professional knowledge and attend and conduct in-service courses. She will belong to and aid a single professional association and accept its rulings once a case has been fairly heard. She will attempt to play some part in the life of her local community and will be fully conversant with and occasionally help with adult education programmes at the community resource centre to which she is attached.

She will assist with the training and supervision of young entrants to the profession, especially those undergoing practice or those who are in their probationary years.

She will recognise that, as pupils get older, they will begin to move away from their immediate locality and she will accept that part of her work will need to be done at field centres or more distant resource centres, and she will make herself available for this.

She will be ready to take her place as tutor panel chairperson if elected, and to undertake the demanding duties of that role for two years.

She will, in other words, see herself, her work and her responsibilities in the same way as do doctors, dentists, architects, lawyers, accountants and clergy, by meeting the different needs of clients in varying ways, in many places, at various times. She will then more than earn her professional status. She will have a status which will be beyond dispute and of which she can be proud.

There will be times when her social role is dominant. Her 'subject teacher' or 'general teacher' role will be subservient to the work she does in helping the child's personal and social development and in helping his family carry out its functions in making this development happy, secure and long-lasting.

Many will see this strong shift in emphasis within the role as being quite as revolutionary as the tutor's progression to full professional status. In reality the two will be closely linked. The ability, willingness and requirement always to take into account the personal developmental needs of each child within the family will bring her into direct contact with the family and require her to give advice and make decisions that will rank as professional work in any occupational league.

It is not, on the other hand, quite so revolutionary as it might seem. Effective teachers who see the development of the whole child as part of their remit are already conscious of the need for their pupil to be happy and to be relieved of worries with which, at his age, he is unable to cope. They try to keep in touch with parents and other people or organisations who are concerned with the child's whole welfare. But there are, within the school-based system, severe limits on how far these aspects of the work can be taken even if the need is apparent and understood and there is the ability and desire to move in that direction. Even those schools which lay great emphasis on pastoral work and which organise personal groups in the care of personal tutors who 'move up' with their groups from year to year, are restricted by the resources they can devote to this work – particularly resources of time and manpower. They see the need but are unable to do all that they would like to do to meet it. The priority in the school system as a whole is for academic progress. A school's 'success' is still measured in terms of reading ages, numeracy levels, test results, examinations passed and grades achieved. Unbelievable as it sounds, in Britain schools are ranked in performance 'leagues' to see which ones are 'high' and which are 'low'!

It is really the wrong way around. If a choice has to be made between the teacher as social worker or as instructor, then that of social worker will come first. But the choice is not so clear-cut. The tutors in the new system of education will be both. In many cases and perhaps for several generations these tutors and their successors will be social workers first and, with the time and energy they have left, traditional 'teachers' second. This ratio of one sub-role to another will vary between different localities within one nation and between nations themselves and will change from time to time.

The priorities must be this way around. No child, whether three or thirteen, is going to do his 'best work' or study to his full potential if he is neglected, abused or unsupported at home and bullied, ostracised or frightened at school. Unless these social problems are sorted out first, the rest can be forgotten: they will, even given great personal effort and national cost, achieve little. At worst they will be counter-productive.

A personally sensitive and expertly trained personal tutor who has known a family since before her pupil's birth will be in a propitious position to help. She will detect problems at an early stage and, in many cases, prevent their worsening. Viewed crudely, from a mercenary standpoint, this could save money for the state by reducing the budget for dealing with the consequences of unobserved or long-neglected problems. The money saved could be used to further the teaching-children-without-schools approach. All would gain from the expertise of a tutor able to intervene effectively, at an early stage, in those matters which affect the happiness of her pupils. Many such matters will originate in the home; the personal tutor should be aware of these, and, unobtrusively, be able to help.

The demands of the role will be great, and it could be argued that the stress suffered by the personal tutor will match that of the teacher in the school-based system. But the stress for the tutor will have a different origin because it will not be generated by the system. It will not be stress born of rising frustration in the workplace. It will be stress arising from the understandable and inevitable concerns and demands of interested parents, and it will be coming from an area over which the tutor herself has considerable control. If she sees that a course of action needs to be followed, she can follow it.

Dealing successfully with parent pressure, over-demand or even intimidation will require a range of skills that will be covered in the tutor's long period of professional training. It will lead to a level of stress with which any professional person, making her own decisions, has to deal and for which she will be prepared and paid. The stress itself is not necessarily a bad thing. It is when it becomes the severe, ongoing stress of frustration, particularly the stress arising from the incompetence, favouritism or sheer insensitivity of those in superior positions that it induces illness. The same is true of the stress attributable to the very nature of a system which dictates from a distance what can and cannot be done to make the lives of local children happier.

Any headteacher in post for six months soon learns that 'difficult' parents are a fact of life and she usually learns – again, 'in post' – to relate to those parents in such a way that at least some benefits accrue from most encounters with them. She knows that the out-and-out 'troublemaker' group is, in most localities, very small indeed, and that most 'difficult' parents are motivated in their actions by a commendable concern for their children. Others, she realises, have 'hidden' reasons for their attitude which they are unable or unwilling to disclose to a teacher who is little known to them.

Sometimes the matters raised are personal and are concerned with intimate relationships within the family which are affecting the child's attitude to and performance in school. The headteacher is limited in what she can do even when the subject is first raised by the parent, but she can listen and talk, or tactfully suggest the intervention of outside agencies if this seems appropriate.

Usually, however, the 'difficult' parent is objecting to how a child is being treated in school. There may be concern at how and what he is being taught, which examinations or subjects he should be taking, 'unreasonable' homework quantities, or which class or group he should be in. These are matters with which a competent headteacher working in the school-based system learns to deal, and which are within her remit. It can be a satisfying part of the job at times, and the headteacher can at least console herself with the thought that, unlike some parents who are never seen in school from one year's end to the next, these 'difficult' parents have some interest in their child's schooling and are anxious to discuss the problem with her or, in less pleasant terms, confront her with it!

Fundamental differences between the school-based system and the teaching-without-schools approach will mean that the personal tutor will inherit many of these 'headteacher' duties. Some concerns or complaints will disappear along with the schools which create them, but others will inevitably arise, and the tutor will be trained to deal with these. She will develop an acceptable, reassuring 'desk-side manner', as opposed to the 'bedside manner' of the general medical practitioner.

There may be parent pressure of the kind the headteacher faced: a wish for the child to follow this or that route or course rather than the one considered best for the child by the personal tutor and her colleagues. There may be threats to remove the child from the group, to complain to the panel chairperson, or to sue for negligence or personal abuse. But the incidence of such threats should be small as the tutor and tutor-panel will have been chosen by the parent and the relationship gradually built up between tutor and parent will be a long, ongoing and close one. The charge of negligence will be unlikely to arise out of the blue and, if it does materialise, will be a problem facing many professional people in society today. If it is used in excess it is a problem which society itself needs to address. If the protection afforded the member by her professional association is inadequate then the state, if it wishes the work of that profession to continue, must interest itself quickly: the lawyers must not be allowed to run riot.

The tutor may encounter resentment from parents at what they see as the tutor's intrusion into family life, or at being asked, no matter how tactfully, to provide information regarded by them as private and personal. If this arises some of the fault may lie with the tutor in being insensitive or in failing fully to explain why such information will be helpful in meeting the needs of the child. There can be no obligation on the part of the parent to divulge anything except the basic data presently given to school authorities such as date of birth and address, but it will be a highly-skilled part of a tutor's task to make clear how much more can be done for a child's social development, his happiness, his health, and subsequently his academic progress if the tutor is held high in the parent's esteem and is entrusted with ample knowledge of the family in which her pupil is maturing.

There may, rarely, be families whose confidence it is difficult to gain, even when it is made clear that the family's children will be the ultimate beneficiaries of that confidence. But if a tutor is meeting many such families it may indicate that, in her case, there was poor selection for the job followed by inadequate preparation. Or there may have been a failure on the part of the tutor to benefit from experience and a failure of other tutors in her tutor panel to give her adequate help. It will then be the tutor's suitability for her work which will be under scrutiny. But the continuing reluctance of the families to co-operate in the tutoring of their children no matter what efforts are made by the tutor panel must not be held wholly against the personal tutor or the new system in which she works.

An exceptionally difficult part of the tutor's role – if she is ever called upon to perform it – will be noting and acting on suspected abuse of a child within the nuclear or extended family. Here her role will move even further towards that of social worker, but this emphasis will be justified because the welfare of the child has to transcend all other considerations.

It may be that direct and ongoing interest by the tutor in the child's treatment within the family will deter family members from ill-treating the child thoughtlessly i.e. without a deliberate intention to be cruel. But if this is not the case and the abuse is calculated to hurt and is repeated despite protestations, then the personal tutor's first duty will be to the child. She will have received training in what to do, what agencies to inform and employ, what support she can expect and information on the role of the legal advisers within the Professional Tutors Guild. But other family members may, to their immense later relief, be deterred from angry assaults on their children by the knowledge that it would be discovered. This would save them from the shame of facing the tutor or even of appearing in court, losing the child, and finishing in prison.

While anti-social behaviour has to be corrected, there can never be justification for physical or psychological pain being imposed on any child. If the new personal approach to childhood education reduces the incidence of child abuse it will have more than merited its introduction.

7. Curriculum perspective

The new education system will ensure that each child knows well a small group of dependable, supportive personal tutors. Each tutor will share a desire to build a long term, caring relationship with each child in her tutor group and, less intensely, with the other children in her tutor panel.

From this relationship, one that is rooted in a family-like community, will come the child's realisation that an agreed set of social values to which everyone adheres will be to the good of himself and everyone else. Then, as he grows older, he will understand not only that this set of values is the prop on which his society leans heavily, but is one which makes possible peaceful, positive international relationships as well.

To further this understanding, each child's educability level will need to be raised and this development can be helped greatly by prolonged contact with his own personal tutors in a study-conducive environment. This environment will embrace his own study-adapted home, his tutors' homes, study rooms in the community resource centre and the resource centres themselves with their books, pictures, music and computer-assisted learning, and the network of field centres. All will be stimulating and reassuring and all will aid interesting learning: all are factors essential to the raising of educability levels.

These increasingly beneficial contacts will develop gradually over the whole early-education period. The child's seven successive personal tutors, who between them will cover that 14-year period with him, will eventually, as the new system progresses, be people who have themselves benefited from a liberal education and who have come to appreciate its value. Many parents, too, as the generations pass, will have gained in this way and, with the new system involving parents extensively, parents and other family members will add much of value to the learning environment of the child.

But not all parents will have gained from their years at school. They are unlikely to look back on them with pleasure. In the saddest cases they may have developed, through desultory school-based learning experiences, an aversion to education as a whole. Because of this they must be helped to see that the teaching-without-schools approach is quite different from that which they themselves experienced at school. The new system's personal, individualised study programme premise must be capable of demonstrating to such parents that there really are worthwhile alternatives to their own form of schooling. This will be a long process covering, in some cases, several generations. But a start has to be made so that eventually all parents can become deeply and enthusiastically involved in their children's early education. They will have been convinced that what is taught and how it is taught is markedly different from their own school experiences and far more worthwhile.

Each child will experience, perhaps for the first time, and over a long period, the outlook and lifestyle of small groups of society's more generously-educated people. In each new generation children will be able to see alternatives to their own family's way of living and will be free to adapt to any aspects of these alternatives they choose. It is likely to be a process of gradual assimilation of values and of gentle, unhurried changes in lifestyle. This may be considered to be in sharp contrast to some early 11+ scholarship winners in the 1940s and 1950s in the U.K. who abandoned the way of life that had been their families' for generations. Sadly, when this happened, many parents and grandparents were left behind wondering what they had done to lose their child.

Under the school-based system deprivation arises not only from differences in quality between schools and teachers but from differences in the lifestyles and value systems of the families sending their children to those schools. The subculture of which a child is a part is a major factor in determining his educability, i.e. in determining "how well he does at school." Teachers cannot change the value systems of other adults, and it can be argued that they should not even try to do so as it would be an impertinence and it is not part of their brief. But they have a responsibility to take into account those aspects of any subculture which deny or lessen a child's lifetime opportunities and to do what they can to compensate for those factors.

Against such a background, the cries for 'equality of opportunity' for children within the school-based system which are heard from politicians are meaningless. Many politicians have no in-depth knowledge of education anyway, and, if they do have such knowledge and appreciate the problems faced by teachers in schools and know the sociological meaning of 'educability', their cries are hypocritical and damaging. They must know that equality of opportunity cannot be externally imposed, and so cannot come from a school-based system, especially if, within that system, there are keenly selective and exclusively expensive schools whose sub culture and facilities are light-years away from those found in state schools in many inner city districts and disadvantaged rural areas.

Such movement towards equality in education as is possible in a society which is itself unequal is unlikely to be achieved in the school system. It is much more likely to be achieved if children are exposed gradually and gently to sub-cultures which emphasise and demonstrate the importance of learning and the value of the arts.

The personalised approach inherent in teaching-children-without-schools, where all children can meet individually and get to know informally and often people who themselves appreciate the importance of education, is much more likely to succeed.

But it will take time, patience and hard work. It will be a slow process. But a start has to be made somewhere, and soon: there is no virtue in standing back, wringing hands and crying "It can't be done".

The child must feel that he can depend, long term, on adults who will care for him, protect him, listen to him and love him. Given this his educability level will rise provided he finds that what he is taught is of interest, relevance and value to him in his life and is within his capabilities. He will use stimulating material, much of which will be of his own choosing, and this will be the rationale behind and form the basis of a personally-devised and supervised individual study programme.

Consideration of these factors needs to be undertaken before a start is made on drawing up a curriculum. Indeed, it could be argued that the traditional 'curriculum' is a thing of the past and that we should no longer think in terms of a 'curriculum' at all. The notion of 'curriculum' binds pupils, parents and teachers to the past making them think of 'subjects' and 'syllabus', and tempts them to shy away from meeting children's true needs. "But we can't do that, it's not on the curriculum...." "We have the prescribed syllabus to get through ... ..." Can't we? Have we? Who says?

Yet, whatever else is in the new curriculum, stress will need to be laid on the transmission of a set of values. This must be embedded in the material presented to children so that those values become part of their everyday lifestyle. These will include the notion that education is valuable and enjoyable and not something that one is conscripted into for set hours each day until adulthood brings release.

It is strange to suggest that the school-based system has undermined the value of education. Ironically, by its compulsory nature and its perceived lack of relevance to and even isolation from life, it has often strengthened a subcultural resistance to education *per se*. This is despite education being the only acceptable, credible and socially acceptable force (as opposed, for example, to gambling or crime) which can offer a change to the very lifestyle of many of those who disregard it or who try to avoid it altogether. At a thoroughly cynical level, one might even say that the very subcultural groups who most need an excellent education are offered one that is indifferent and which would not be tolerated by more favoured families. The result is that the least well-educated remain the least well-educated. They can pin their hopes on a national lottery win!

It has the basis of genuine tragedy: there are whole groups of young people, in generation after generation, who are inexorably and unthinkingly in opposition to the one force in society which could be instrumental in bettering their lives. This rejection of education, from which the whole of society is ultimately the loser, is much more of a reflection on the current schooling organisation than a condemnation of education as a whole. But these young people are unaware of this nice distinction and see the two as interchangeable: schooling equals education equals disillusionment equals rejection. Then it starts all over again with the next generation.

It is reasonable to expect educationalists to be aware of this dichotomy and to be seeking viable alternatives to a 19th century idea of education which is school and classroom based. But the opposite seems to be the case. In Britain, as recently as 1972-73, a hundred years after the introduction of elementary, authoritarian school-based learning, and with signs of its rejection by mid 20th century teenagers already there for all to see, an extension to schooling was made so that children stayed at school until the age of 16+ instead of 15+. They were to be given more of the same in the same buildings by the same hard-pressed teachers.

This steady, statutory raising of the school-leaving age from 10 in the 1870s to 16 in the 1970s, which has not been confined to Britain, is further evidence that Western society is mesmerised by the idea that teaching the young can take place only in compulsorily-attended purpose-built schools in which teachers work largely alone expending much of their nervous energy and everyone's time in keeping pupils in a tolerable state of order. 'Good discipline' this is called, and it has been the downfall of many kind, clever, concerned, experienced, creative and valuable teachers.

It is possible, but inexcusable, that many in positions of authority in education do not appreciate the significance of what is happening in the schools and therefore continue to support the school-based structure. Others may have a vested interest in maintaining the status quo because educational administration in one guise or another, within or outside the school, offers a highly-paid career free of the stress of the day to day classroom-teaching advocated by the very establishment to which they belong. Those who hold sway here are emulated by those promotion-seeking teachers who, by taking on more and more administrative work, reduce their hours in the classroom and increase both their salaries and their power. They become, in their own eyes and those of others, 'more important' than the classroom-teaching practitioner. It is an expensive, highly frustrating and divisive nonsense. It is connived at, if not openly encouraged, by central, local and school government, and is part of a lucrative 'divide and rule the teachers' policy which has evolved relentlessly over a century or more.

So serious has the British situation become that it is at last being governmentally addressed in a consultative Green Paper (December 1998), with proposals made to reward those outstanding teachers who elect to stay at work in the classroom rather than seek 'promotion' in administration. But the proposals are partial and, even if they were implemented fully, would be fraught with the century-old difficulties of fairness in the selection of such teachers. And, just as discouraging, they accept for the foreseeable future an education dependent on the old school and classroom-based teacher and pupil formula.

At one time this hierarchical, divisive scenario was mainly secondary-school based, but it has moved into schools for younger children as various 'posts of responsibility' have been established which lower the importance of the vital task of teaching the very children for whom the schools exist. Where schools, for example in rural villages, are too small to be 'viable' and *ipso facto* too small to support an elaborate hierarchy within the staff, they are closed. Even the youngest children are then transferred to larger schools by being transported to and from their own villages. This can be both distressing and time-wasting for the children and does little to help local communities maintain their identities and lifestyles. For instance it was reported in *The Times Educational Supplement* of 9 July 1999 that almost 500 small schools (i.e. schools having less than 100 pupils) had been closed in the U.K. in the previous five years despite evidence that they had provided a high quality of education.

This procedure is justified also because it is held that the small two, three or four teacher school is 'inefficient' in terms of overall cost per pupil and too narrow in the diversity of curriculum and facilities it can offer. Yet often the small village school has been one of the few redeeming features of the 19th century school-based system. It has given much in terms of the close relationship established between pupils, parents, teachers and members of the local community.

But this has counted for little as the education system has become more bureaucratic and accountants more influential. Estate agents have moved in and well-built village schools and school houses have been sold as 'desirable residences' or 'ideal for light industry' and lost to the local community for ever.

But the close relationships of that 'tiny school' mode will be vital in the new, small-group system of personal tutoring. The organisation that emerges and the value-rich curriculum which accompanies it will maximise opportunities for children to assimilate ideas and create activities of their own choosing. It will introduce them to new interests. Overall this will be socially acceptable, personally pleasurable and practically useful.

8. Curriculum guidance

Against the background of each child's needs and capabilities, and the parents' wishes and opinions, and what the nation state can afford and is prepared to provide, some concensus has to be reached on the guidance to be offered to parents and personal tutors on what might be borne in mind when a child's individual study programme is compiled. There are many possible approaches to this guidance outline and the one offered here is seen only as a starting point.

Two important considerations are (i) the child's individual development, which is paramount, and (ii) the need for this development to take place within a social environment that is secure, stable, fair, law-abiding and enriching. Security and stability in the child's world must be assured even though the wider world in which he exists is in a state of continual change.

Given consensus on this, it is likely that there will be six elements working in conjunction with each other. Five of these can be seen as part of an 'open' curriculum, while the working-out of the sixth will be 'hidden' or at least much less obvious. But there will be 'hidden' aspects in all six elements in that goals other than those that are immediately apparent and specific will be present.

All will have a common purpose in that they will be helping to raise the level of each child's educability, and helping to establish a set of social values that will make possible his happy life in an ordered and increasingly international society. The six elements will not necessarily be of equal worth to all pupils, nor of equal worth to any one pupil at all stages of his childhood. Neither, probably, will they be equally highly regarded by all parents and tutors. But none will be valueless to any of these parties.

The six elements, as set out in the Charter for the Central Audio-Visual Education Library (CAVEL) on page 97, will be:

(1) literacy and numeracy

(2) combined studies and/or general knowledge
(3) the arts
(4) leisure and recreation
(5) community, national and international service
(6) national and international social philosophy

(1) Literacy and numeracy

The first element will be a study of language and mathematics to a level of literacy and numeracy considered necessary for a child living in Western society in the 21st century.

Work in the English language, or the language native to the child, which will begin at birth, will emphasise the development of (i) non-verbal communication; (ii) listening, talking, reading and writing skills; and (iii) enjoyment of stories, well-illustrated books, reading, personal writing, radio, television and CAVEL stories, plays and films, plus the parents', grandparents' and tutor's personal contributions.

Work in mathematics will also emphasise enjoyment as discoveries are made and problems solved. There will be high input here from CAVEL's lesson units, and a comparison can be made with the excellent material for use by teachers currently broadcast for schools by, for example, British radio and television.

A pupil will not necessarily continue this basic study for all fourteen years of early education. If the tutors of a panel agree that a pupil has reached a satisfactory utilitarian level, or when they and a child's parents accept that his educability is of such a low order that he is unlikely to make further significant progress and that his time could be better spent in other pursuits, they will discontinue the study of these two areas *as particular entities.* However, both will be continued incidentally by personal tutors and, in some cases, parents.

With other pupils, too, once basic literacy and numeracy are attained, progress will appear to the student to be largely subsidiary to what is being studied. But in effect it will be substantial: there will be natural development in these two sectors arising from work done in other areas of the curriculum and this will continue until the child moves on to middle education at age fourteen.

Systematic and more advanced work in language and mathematics, where each again will be seen as a subject in its own right, will be undertaken as soon as it is relevant to the pupil's needs and is within his capability. Most pupils will be required to opt for the continuation of these subjects in the middle education stage (ages 14 to 15) and in later education (16 to 17+). These two stages are outlined in Chapter 5, *The Next Stage* (page 131). All children, throughout the early education stage, will enjoy and spend much time on literature and drama and, in this way, be helped immeasurably in the development of their language skills.

Figure 3. The curriculum from birth to 14 years.

Open curriculum : one third.	Seven two-year stages.	OPEN:
	Birth to ... age 14 years	Concentrates on growing familiarity and love of: music – heard and played; stories – heard and told; pictures – seen and imagined, drawn and painted; printed word – read, written, listened to when read. Growing mastery and enjoyment of learning skills; competence in all aspects of language and number work; reference and computer skills; increasing knowledge of a gradually widening environment; personal health and safety.

Hidden curriculum: two thirds.	In seven two-year stages from birth to fourteenth birthday.	HIDDEN
	Birth to ... age 14 years	From birth the child receives love, affection, respect, concern, interest, security through stable relationships with parent(s) and fully professional personal tutors. The child develops values of trust, reliability, honesty, concern for others and the environment, respect for others, appreciation of what is done for him, his need to give, and to play a constructive part in the community. The child appreciates: the natural environment, music, art, literature, drama, other cultures, value of hobbies, sport, travel, friendship. The child acquires: lifelong values through examples shown by others whom he respects, from those emanating from literature and history, by the realisation that education and life develop together and that much of what is worthwhile and enjoyable is compatible with conservation of resources. The child moves away from concern for self to concern for others.

(2) Combined studies and/or general knowledge

The second element will be the development, informally and by means of an interdisciplinary approach, of the child's awareness and appreciation of his environment. In the very early years, from birth to seven, it will encompass the limited and local environment around the child's and tutor's homes. Later, with more input from CAVEL, the community resource centre, and field centres, studies will be widened geographically and historically, and will introduce aspects of the general sciences that can be related to these areas. Usually, with parents' cognisance, this will not be seen as a traditional, subject-organised approach and will not be structured in that way. Such highly-structured 19th and 20th century formality, involving the often arbitrary separation of material into subjects, is unlikely, in the new system, to begin much before middle education. There will be some pupils for whom this division will never be desirable or practised, and others for whom a formal, subject-based approach could come earlier. Both groups, however, are likely to be small minorities, but both can be catered for in the new system by working with CAVEL.

(3) The arts

This third element will be the largest of the whole curriculum and could be as large as all the other elements put together. It will help every child gain pleasure from literature, music, drama, arts and crafts, beginning at birth, and will interest parents too. The bias will be unashamedly strong and the pupil's awareness, experience and enjoyment of these spheres will be increased deliberately as he matures, as will his skill and appreciation.

Literacy will have high priority throughout the curriculum and all tutors will see themselves as personally responsible for, and skilled in, its furtherance. Much will be achieved through the pleasure of reading. The immensely humanising potential of studying, at whatever level is appropriate, carefully chosen and sympathetically discussed books written by a range of authors past and present at home and abroad, will be applicable to all children, although the difficulty of the literature studied and the depth at which it is understood will vary greatly and depend on the personal tutor's own width of reading and her ability to assess her pupils' comprehension levels and personal needs. As in so many other areas of her work, success will lie with her ability to select from all that is available and match it to the requirements of her pupils.

Particularly valuable in this sector of the curriculum, but of value in the others, too, will be accurately and sensitively written autobiographies and biographies in either arts or science, either contemporary or historical. These will feature in most children's individual study programmes. Stories of the lives of men and women of all nationalities and times who have helped mankind will be used often in their literary and other studies. Sometimes and, as always, at tutor's and parents' discretion, the effects on humanity of evil acts, and a study of the lives of the perpetrators, will be considered, as will possible reasons for such evil and ways in which it might in future be averted.

While extensive lists of books, with guidelines as to suitability and use will be supplied on request by CAVEL, tutors and parents will accept or reject recommendations as they consider best, and will add titles of their own choosing. There will be no rigidly-structured courses designed for whole age-groups of children, nor 'set books' on which children will later be 'examined'. For instance, no child will be asked to read a novel, poem or play in order to pass a two-hour paper in English literature. The pupil will hear a poem recited, read a novel or biography or see a film or take part in a drama because it is one of the many recommended to him by someone whose opinions he values and trusts, or because he discovered it for himself in the resource centre library or bookshop, or because he was introduced to it in a CAVEL lesson unit included in his personal study programme.

Tutors, parents and pupils might or might not talk or write about or analyse the work afterwards. It will be for the tutor sensitively to appraise the desirability of this, just as she will consider other work options for individual members of her group.

As a preference for particular books, poems, plays, films, music and art is so dependent on a combination of individual ability, interests and taste, there will be few if any common courses. It will be here that a tutor's fine competence in compiling individual and flexible study programmes will be so important. It is also where the tutor's growing knowledge of what material is available, and what can be included profitably in each pupil's programme, will be vital. It will be where a tutor's task will reach a peak. It will be one of those many times when her work will be as professionally demanding as it is satisfying. It will not be measurable in pounds, dollars, euros, or any other common currency: it will be beyond price.

(4) Leisure and recreation

The fourth element of the curriculum will introduce the child to the widest practicable range of other recreational opportunities. While many will be chosen by the child himself, there will be encouragement to try pursuits previously unknown to him.

There will be special emphasis on those activities likely to meet leisure needs years ahead. Included in many study-programmes of older children will be opportunities for foreign travel and demonstrations of how this can be undertaken, often with parents, on a low budget. Similarly, all chances of inviting children and their families from other countries and entertaining them and learning from them will be taken eagerly.

Included in many programmes will be the use of facilities at the community resource centre, such as playing fields, tennis courts, gymnasia, auditoria and music rooms. These will be available for individual use or for group or team events. For team games two tutors might combine groups, and at the same time will be able to enhance the social value of the work.

Use will be made of facilities at middle and later education colleges, while the network of field centres in the home country and abroad will benefit pupils and families.

(5) Community, national and international service

This fifth element will be a gradual introduction to community service. In the very early years this will be limited to finding out about groups in society who help pupils and their families, but will not preclude, even at this stage, practical consideration of the daily needs of others, and of how many people can be helped in quite simple ways.

This work will be steadily increased until, between ages ten and fourteen, pupils will move into the community with parents and personal tutors to offer practical help to other people in specific ways. Initially this may mean, for example, the occasional clearing of rubbish from the neighbourhood, but later the work will evolve until there is a regular performance of services on which less capable members of society can rely. The importance of this *reliance* will be stressed continually.

There will be an element of self-help throughout the early education years. Children will be responsible for their own belongings and the tidiness of their rooms, and of the resource centre rooms they use. Then, later, there will be a combination of self-help and community service as the resource centre will, throughout the year, be offering support not only to the child's own tutor group but to other tutor groups and panels and to the wider community as well. Thus the help given will be reciprocated. As they grow older children will give help to others by collecting money or goods for communities at home or abroad whose need is great.

(6) Social philosophy

The sixth and last element will comprise much of the 'hidden' curriculum and will encourage the growth of a set of social attitudes that encompass the major values of the pupil's Western society. These will include the need for the pupil to make good use of his abilities for the benefit of others as well as himself; to appreciate the value of the education he is being offered, and to respect the legitimate rights of fellow citizens. As far as possible he will be helped to accept responsibility for his own life and to make a contribution to the lives of other people.

Much of the tuition needed to promote this social philosophy will be incidental. At times attitudes and values will be passed on almost casually. Such inculcation has a greater chance of succeeding via the new personal group system than under the old school-based one. The values will be fostered in the groups in the same way as they are in a caring, aware and socially responsible family. The values will be strengthened by examples set in tutors' homes and families, by assistance given to parents, and by the choice of reading material made in the different areas chosen for study. All will be reinforced by means of the carefully-made programmes seen and heard on public radio and television and from the more specifically-aimed multimedia material emanating from CAVEL. All this will be followed by interpretations and criticisms from tutors and in discussions in their personal groups.

The unfolding of this social philosophy will be the very core of the 'hidden' curriculum: tutors will know that its development forms an integral part of the other five elements. While it will appear to be described only briefly in the brochures published by tutor panels and receive less page space than the other elements, tutors and parents will know it is there and that it is as important as the other segments of the curriculum. Such a philosophy will lie behind tutors' daily work with their pupils and with their pupils' families. It will help each child to know that:

- He is secure, loved, consulted and important.
- He is not pressurised by being placed in unreasonable competition with other children.
- Study can be of value and enjoyable in itself.
- Other people are important and their happiness has to be considered.
- Finding acceptance in a social group requires sustained effort and, at times, compromise.
- Through guided choice he is being helped to develop interests that can last a lifetime.
- His happiness and that of others depends on aggression being controlled and violence avoided.

Tutors' responsibilities and skills

The ways in which these aims are achieved will be determined by the personal tutor in collaboration with her colleagues, her pupils' parents and, in the case of older pupils, the pupils themselves. The approach will be different from child to child, tutor to tutor and family to family. The blanket exhortations and admonitions of necessity made and so often resented or ignored in the old school-based system will be inappropriate and unnecessary in the new one.

How available time might be allocated between the six categories at different stages of the child's 14 years of early education is suggested in the table
(Figure 4) below. Variation on this example will be great and will depend partly on (i) perception of individual pupil need and (ii) parents' and tutors' evaluation of the work covered by each category.

Figure 4. Assessment of pupil need within an agreed curriculum.

Six (linked) categories of personal growth and social development in first 14 years of life.	Possible tutor allocation of increasing study time available as child matures, in 7 age groups:						
	0-1	2-3	4-5	6-7	8-9	10-11	12-13
1. Literacy and numeracy	30	65	95	105	95	70	35
2. General knowledge	15	25	45	55	65	70	80
3. Appreciation of the arts	40	80	105	115	145	170	200
4. Leisure and recreation	5	15	30	35	45	70	90
5. Community service	5	5	10	20	25	40	60
6. Social philosophy	5	10	15	20	25	30	35
Study time (from base 100)	100	200	300	350	400	450	500

Notes on table:

• Categories and ages equate to those suggested for the teaching-without-schools programme earlier (p.65 and p.66) and may differ from those chosen by other tutors and
parents working in different circumstances.
• Base figures are illustrative of relative allocation and do not refer to specific periods
(i.e. hours or days).
• Study time means all time given to activities from which the baby or child learns about
himself or other people or his widening environment.
• Such study time will vary greatly from day to day, child to child, and stage to stage.

Notes on six categories:

1. While emphasising reading and pre-reading activity, this includes acquisition of other
skills required for enjoyment of life and service to the community.
2. In addition to factual knowledge, considers what has been *and what might have been*
done in his culture – with gradual evaluation of same.
3. Encourages child to explore music, literature and art, to discern beauty, and to create
beauty in work of his own making.
4. Includes progress towards a healthy lifestyle and considers importance of diet, exercise, routine check-ups, and wide-ranging interests.
5. Helps with appreciation of his family, then of the wider community and how he can
help, and thoughts of a future family of his own.
6. Promotes observation of all around him – including variations of behaviour and what
is 'right' and 'wrong' – and of selection, appraisal, choice, decision-making, and emu-
lation of 'most worthy' activities.

The most effective means for the tutor and the one most likely to establish good relationships with pupils and families – and therefore the one most likely to secure an acceptance of the required social values – will be the professional freedom given to the tutor to make decisions herself. She will promote those values that she is certain she believes in, those that she is confident of advancing, and those which she knows have helped her personally through her childhood, adolescence and university years. Suitably modified and judiciously introduced, they will help her pupils too.

When, rarely, her partiality in tutoring methods conflict with what is best for her pupil or with the justifiable demands of his family, it will be the pupil's needs, always, which take priority. Similarly, while the tutor will usually see her pupils' needs and those of society as complementary, she will, where divergence occurs, put her pupil's interests first even if her action brings disapproval on herself.

In this way a fully professional relationship between personal tutor, child and family will be built and maintained. The basis of the tutor's professionalism will be (a) that the client's interests will always be paramount, and (b) that the level of skill and judgement required in her work will be of the high order rightly demanded of a professional person, and (c) that those skills and the knowledge needed will be kept up to date.

9. Personal tutors

The professional, personal family tutor will be the key figure in the whole teaching-children-without-schools scheme, and her twenty-strong personal group of pupils will be the key unit.

For the new system to begin, experienced, qualified teachers in the present school-based system will, in one county or local education authority, be asked to volunteer for service. They will be offered a one-year period of professional retraining and, on successful completion of this, will begin work as professional personal tutors in a tutor panel.

There will be no pressure brought on any teacher to retrain or to join the new scheme. Indeed, the opposite will be the case for, with the first groups of retrainees, classteachers will be selected not only for their previous excellent professional relationships with children and the high level of their teaching skills, but for the degree of enthusiasm they have for the new approach. A lukewarm "I'll give it a try", or "It'll make a change," or "It can't be any worse than what we've got already," will not suffice.

When the scheme is under way there will be careful selection of candidates by standing committees consisting of resource centre wardens, representatives of professional associations, educationalists and parents. Selected candidates will need to be in agreement with the basic underlying philosophy of the new model – that the child's welfare is paramount. His babyhood and childhood must be happy and secure and his need to be wanted fully satisfied. He will be helped to acquire amenable companionship and a range of enjoyable interests. The support of an individual personal tutor will be vital.

To achieve this, each child will be taught partly within the family group, partly on his own by his tutor, and partly within small groups of children. The composition of these groups will vary from time to time according to the tutor's assessment of the best arrangement for any particular activity and the nature of the venue. Groups may consist of two or three children or of the whole of the tutor's group of twenty similarly-aged pupils.

In such specific activities as the production of a play, musical or film, several tutor-groups can combine – perhaps groups from different tutor-panels – and use the drama facilities of the community resource centre for rehearsals, and its hall and stage for any final performances. Similar combinations of groups or parts of groups can be made for team games and, again, the resource centre facilities can be reserved for each tutor's priority use.

To succeed in her work, the tutor will require a range of abilities and skills and extensive knowledge of child development and family relationships. These attributes will fall into six main categories.

First she will need to have adequate knowledge of each of the twenty children in her care. This will include medical history, likes and dislikes, fears and worries, intellectual abilities (especially in relation to the development of literacy and numeracy), special interests, ability to establish and maintain relationships with other children, previous school or similar experience, and family composition and background in terms of the support that parents and other family members are able and willing to give. She will also need to be aware of the suitability for study purposes of family housing, details of siblings and any particular strengths and weaknesses in the family unit.

Second she will need to be fully informed about all those in the family or the immediate neighbourhood who are likely to have a strong influence on the child's development. She will know about parental occupations and qualifications, schooling, and attitudes to education and its intrinsic value. She will learn whether the child has his own bedroom, books, tv, video machine, computer, pets, part-time jobs, spending money, and whether he is allocated household duties reasonable for his age. She will find out about parental attitudes to the upbringing of their children and of children in general; whether the family regime is strict, lenient, consistent, loving, democratic or autocratic and whether there is a helpful household routine which will aid the child's study and her own professional tutorial work.

Third, she will need to have expertise in many aspects of child development. She must be able to use this in her work, and be able to explain to parents what the normal patterns of development are as well as the extent to which they can vary between children. She will explain to parents the differences between maturation and learning. She will point out that the first is the natural propensity for children – indeed all human beings – to grow in an ordered sequence of stages: that these developments cannot be taught and are not induced by variations in the child's environment. She will stress here the contrast with learning and will show, gradually, how example, experience, stimulation and environmental factors will help a child to learn, and that prolonged lack of these will lead to long-term, serious, avoidable deprivation.

This passing on of her knowledge to parents will be essential if they are to maximise the help they give her in her work with their child. She will be well read on motivation to learn, developing attention spans, powers of concentration, childhood perceptions of the world, the growth of memory, the acquisition of language, the meaning of intelligence, and the nature of educability.

She must be able to explain to parents how these and other factors combine, with many others – and with incredible intricacy – to form their child's unique personality. Above all she will stress the importance of these early years of life and the fact that they come only once. Knowing this might increase the willingness of many parents to increase the time and care they give to their children especially if they are assisted by the state – as they are in this teaching-without-schools proposal – to do this.

Fourth, she will need to have extensive knowledge of the mass of material available from all the new sources and of how it can be quickly located and referenced. She will need the editing skills necessary to compile logical, carefully-graded and attractive study programmes from that material and the ability to present it in a manageable, attractive form for the use of pupil and parent.

Fifth, she must be able to meet the current needs of each child through the excellence of the individual study programmes she provides. Within the programme she will organise many activities. These may be formal or informal, at home or elsewhere, with or without parental participation, with individual students or with groups of various sizes. They will be based on work that is academic in nature or craft-based or sport-based, and work which is focussed primarily on the child's intellectual development or his social development. The professional tutor, although appearing at times to be working informally – even haphazardly – will, in effect, be systematic in her planning; she will be observing and recording child and parental reaction with a view to later adaptation and continuation of the study programme. Then, within the tutor panel, a tutor may,

Figure 5. Group organisation and the child's changing needs.

The Family:
With professional guidance from tutors as needed, the family gives love, security and early learning opportunities in the home.

The Personal Tutor and Personal Group: both help each child to associate increasingly with other children and adults in pairs or in groups of three or four within the personal group. The child moves to another group and another personal tutor every two years and the parents are closely involved throughout the fourteen years of early education.

The Tutor Panel: (seven personal groups and eight tutors) helps the child, as he grows older, to associate with larger groups in drama, choirs, games and excursions, and to learn how to give and take. Parental involvement continues through all seven two-year stages.

The Community Resource Centre: provides study space, learning facilities, gymnasium, pool, stage, hall and other learning opportunities for child, friends and family.

The Field Centre: extends the child's horizon by offering day and boarding facilities for families and groups further and further afield - including the use of field centres abroad.

The Central Audio-Visual Education Library: with its immense resources, provides much carefully graded teaching material to enable the changing needs of the individual developing child to be met.

Other Opportunities: As the child grows older the value of meetings, courses, conferences, camps and exchanges will be noted and acted on by child, parent and tutor.

if she feels easier doing so, work with a colleague for part of the time. In some ways there will be advantages in this – for instance in a male and female partnership or one between an experienced and a newly-qualified tutor, or one which meets particular parental preferences, or in a study unit which calls for specialised knowledge, experience or skills.

Sixth will be an ability gently to persuade. There will be times when tutor and parent differ on what is best for the child. Examples of this abound in the present school-based system, such as when a parent has unrealistic aspirations for a child and wants the child to attempt courses and examinations which are beyond his abilities and later lead only to disappointment. This disappointment will bring feelings of dissatisfaction with the school on the part of the parent, resentment and loss of self-confidence on the part of the pupil, and sadness on the part of the disregarded teacher.

The need for the personal tutor to be able to argue rationally and to persuade kindly but firmly will be essential in the new system. Personal tutor and parent will be in close and frequent contact in the building-up, amendment and execution of personal study-programmes over a two-year period. While, eventually, the parent's wishes will have to be respected, a tutor will need to have an understanding of the parent's position and of how she can present, effectively, viable alternatives that will, at the very least, be considered seriously.

Much time will need to be spent during initial tutor-training sessions on child-parent-tutor relationships, and then again later in in-service courses arranged by the tutors' own professional association via panel chairpersons and resource and field centre wardens.

The tutor's usual pattern of work will be to tutor a few pupils at a time – perhaps three or four – for an hour or ninety minutes, three or four times each week. This will be shorter than existing teacher-class contact time in schools, but is likely to be of greater value than the customary thirty class hours in which the average pupil gets less personal attention from the teacher. In a class of thirty the highly-able or highly-disruptive pupils can monopolise much of a teacher's time to the detriment of the majority of lower-profile children.

Each tutor will be working within a tutor panel and will have the moral and physical support of her colleagues in that panel. Often she will make use of their knowledge, experience and expertise, especially that of those personal tutors who cared for her pupils at earlier stages, and that of the panel chairperson. She will enjoy colleagues' company when she chooses to be with them.

But always she will be her own mistress. She will decide her own actions in her professional work. Her responsibility will be to her clients and that responsibility will be uppermost. To gain acceptance in the new profession of tutoring each tutor will need to be highly skilled, compassionate and reliable. She will then be seen as an educational practitioner on a par with members of other professions. Her work will be of prime importance in society because she will be helping a group of parents in the upbringing of their young children. Nothing can be more important than that if a compassionate, well-balanced international community is to be developed in the 21st century.

10. Personal groups

Most family personal tutors will care for approximately twenty pupils for a period of two years. The exceptions will be tutor panel chairpersons who, for a period of two years, will have no personal group of their own. In addition to their other duties, chairpersons will aid other tutors, as required, in the tutor panel. A panel will consist of seven tutor groups.

The personal group will be made up of some twenty children whose ages fall within one of seven bands:

Band one:	birth to 24 months
Band two:	2 to 3 years inclusive
Band three:	4 to 5 years inclusive
Band four:	6 to 7 years inclusive
Band five:	8 to 9 years inclusive
Band six:	10 to 11 years inclusive
Band seven:	12 to 13 years inclusive

The children will be taught individually by tutor or parent or both, in small groups of three or four by tutor or parent or a nominee of these, or in larger groups i.e. ten, fifteen or twenty, for drama, sports or some educational visits. Larger groups will be taught by tutor and parents or by other tutors or those parents who have specific knowledge or skills in the areas required. Suitably-qualified and interesting outside speakers, demonstrators, instructors, and sportspersons, all of whom must be able to relate interestingly to children, will be invited to help an individual child or a whole personal group.

Although a sound knowledge of child development from birth to fourteen years will be required of all tutors, each will tend to specialise in one or two adjoining two-year age-groups. The skills called for in helping parents in the very early months of a child's life will be different from many of those needed to help pupils who are preparing for their next stage of education in a middle education college at age fourteen. Love, compassion, understanding and respect will be given by all personal tutors to all their pupils no matter what age they are teaching. All tutors will require, in addition, the ability to discern need, recognise teaching opportunities and relate effectively to parents and children. They must be able to persuade, plan, organise, anticipate, explain, illustrate, interpret, develop, examine and assess.

But more will be asked of personal tutors who work primarily in the first two bands: those who help with the development of children in their first four years. Those tutors, more than any other, will be in immediate, long-term, regular contact with parents in their own homes. They will be *helping parents to help their children.*

This area provides one of the major differences between the five to sixteen year state school system (in the UK) and the birth to fourteen years covered by the teaching-without-schools proposals of this book. This new approach regards the first four years as so vital to the happy development of the child – and his prospects for the future – that it brings that stage wholly into the mainstream education system.

The system presented here does not see 'popular', i.e. universal education, for any child, as a process which begins formally at age five (UK) or six (USA). These are arbitrary, administratively convenient points in a child's life and have little meaning beyond that.

There seems to be little disagreement here, and concessions are made already to these statutory ages, at least in the UK, by the national and local government support given to 'pre-schooling' for many under-fives. There are also private nurseries, playgroups and childminders. Church groups, too, are active, and private enterprise initiatives such as The Boots Company's *Books for Babies* project, aid the development of literacy.

Under the teaching-without-schools scheme this work would be brought under one large, protective umbrella. Its virtues would be enhanced and the whole package would be made available to every family on an equal basis. Help would be offered to parents on a regular, reliable, sustained footing by qualified, professional, personal tutors who, although they specialised in the education of babies and very young children, would be an integral part of the whole early education scheme. All the new scheme's facilities and support would be at their disposal, as would in-service training and CAVEL links. They would maintain close contact with the tutors of older children and assist them by offering their expertise. There would be no arbitrary break in the child's education or the personal tutors' work until the fourteen year old child moved on to middle education college. (See figure 16, page 133).

The invaluable assistance now given to families by health and social workers in the child's early months would continue at the present level at least. Help given by grandparents and other relatives, and friends, would be retained with gratitude. All that is personally supportive today would be further encouraged, as would the highly regarded help of voluntary agencies and societies.

To this would be added a strong educational input. This would be for the immediate and long-term benefit of baby and parent and would be to the satisfaction of both: the parent would know that he or she was doing as good a job as possible, and the baby would gain by being given informed (i.e. appropriate) stimulation.

For tutorial help to be effective in what will be, at times, an exceptionally sensitive area, the tutor will need always to be considerate of parents' feelings. These feelings will be an amalgam of love and possessiveness, a determination to protect and a desire to provide. There will be a wish to do what is best for the baby while remaining in control of all that is happening. At times this may lead to a reluctance to take advice, adopt suggestions or examine ideas, followed by a feeling of guilt at the reluctance! All this, and more, family personal tutors must be trained first to recognise and then to allow for.

But many parents will welcome all the advice that is available on ways of stimulating their child and maximising his potential. They will enjoy doing it and will not miss any opportunity to help. They will want to expand their own knowledge and skill and, even where interest appears to be less than whole-hearted, a perceptive tutor will realise that her words are often quietly heeded and her suggestions surreptitiously assimilated.

Responses from most parents are likely to fluctuate as their moods change along with those of the baby. If the baby cries for days, seems to make little progress, and begins to compare unfavourably with highly-achieving babies at the health centre clinic, the parents will be glad of any help. Yet at other times they will seem to be supremely confident and almost indifferent to the tutor's presence and her ideas: "I'm managing very well, thank you. He's coming along fine!"

Others may be influenced unduly by older family members who will relate at length how they brought up their children "without any help of that kind!" and then tell the new mother or father: "And we did all right". But gradually as the nearby, supportive extended family yields further to the more isolated nuclear family, this influence will wane and the need for help increase. Tutors must be mindful of the ways in which social and demographic changes affect attitudes and behaviour and then determine the need for help. They must allow for these factors in planning their work.

But with some families it will be difficult to get a foot across the door. Here there may be animosity towards anyone from 'officialdom' even though tutors, tutor panels and local community resource centres will have been at pains for years to point out that the personal tutor is a professional person in her own right and takes instructions from no one except her parent and child clients: that she acts always in their best interests.

With people in the last group, and with some others, there will be no virtue in pressing. The attractions of the local community resource centre and the helpfulness of its staff will bring in many parents. Then there will be chances to talk, to assist, and to demonstrate the benefits of the new system for everyone.

Indifferent, reluctant and even hostile parents will see when at the centre, and also hear on the grapevine, that many parents and their babies are profiting greatly from the ready availability of support, ideas, companionship and others' expertise. One day they will come on board of their own free will. Much will depend here on the tutor's own professional education, her inherent perspicacity and her acute sense of timing.

Just as there are important matters of which the tutor must be aware, there are points with which the parents need to be familiar. Where parental awareness is weak or non-existent, the personal tutor can do much to strengthen or make known those points. Ten examples, not necessarily in order of importance and certainly not exhaustive, are that:

● Varied stimuli, from numerous sources – such as members of the family other than the mother and father – need, frequently, to be introduced.
● Large sums of money are not necessary for such stimulation to be effective: babies need to be talked to, sung to, shown things, listened to.
● Improvisation is important, inexpensive, and enjoyable for parent and baby. Such 'makeshift' material can produce simple toys and colourful pictures which are then expendable and can be touched, squeezed, thrown about and slobbered over until they are disdainfully rejected for a fresh attraction.
● Similarly, 'educational' visits do not have to be planned weeks in advance with seats booked and tickets bought: the church yard, park, farm or supermarket are all 'educational' to the young child and come free of charge.
● Explaining, in appropriately simple terms, is vital. Even before the child can say 'why, when, who, what, where or how' the knowledgeable, observant parent is ready to offer explanations and reasons relating to everyday activities.
● The gaining of confidence and winning of independence – even at the painful expense of the parent – has to be fostered and encouraged.
● Such gradual moving away from the parents is part of normal development, and that there are helpful 'norms' in this as in other fields.
● Shyness with, or fear of, other people, has to be noted and, kindly, acted upon.
● It is important not to underestimate what a child understands or can do.
● That the development of a healthy lifestyle – in what we eat and drink, and how much we sleep, exercise, and interest ourselves in many things – probably begins much earlier than many people think: certainly before a child reaches the statutory age of formal schooling.

In more practical ways the band one and band two personal tutors will be able to help parents by offering, at appropriate times, to:

- Introduce them, informally, at the resource centre and elsewhere, to the parents of children of a similar age or, preferably in some cases, of children slightly older than their own, i.e. parents who have recently experienced the same stage of development with their own children.
- Help with the organisation of babysitting groups.
- Show how almost anything to hand in house, garden, street or shop can have educational significance for a child and provide enjoyable, purposeful learning opportunities.
- Accompany parents to local libraries, parks, stores and markets to show further simple teaching practices.
- 'Take a turn' at entertaining an infant, in its home or the tutor's, or in the resource centre, while the parent meets others or simply relaxes.
- Arrange short, local visits for groups of parents and their babies or toddlers.
- Awaken an interest in the child for books and pictures, words and colours.
- Interest the child in its immediate environment first by recognition and name, and then by relating it to other significant features in its own life.
- Assess how the child is progressing in relation to an understood maturation sequence – one with which the tutor will be fully conversant: ditto with regard to the acquisition of social skills.
- Introduce the parents to other people who may be able to help with specific and seemingly long-lasting problems that worry the parents.

An important part of any tutor's work, no matter what age she tutors, will be recording progress made and ensuring that this information is available in good time for the next-stage tutor and the tutor panel chairperson. But it is particularly important that this is done meticulously by the band two tutor when her pupils reach their fourth birthday. Parents must be made aware formally – although in practice all will already be aware informally – of any special strengths or of areas where their child needs extra help.

Sometime after the age of four years the child will begin to rely for much of his further progress on experiences undergone or work learned: there will need to be some building on what is now known or on skills now acquired. It would be reasonable, therefore, for the tutor, close to the child's fourth birthday, to assess, with the parents' co-operation, the child's ability to:

- Describe orally, so that others can understand, simple scenes or recent experiences.
- Relate a short chain of events in their order of happening.
- Listen to a simple story and relate its main points.
- Talk about what he would like to do, or hopes to do, in the immediate (or distant) future.

82

- Be familiar with books: their covers, pages, words and pictures, and to appreciate that, when he is being read to, the words and pictures have meaning.
- Recite a nursery rhyme or sing a song, or both.
- Follow one or two simple instructions and remember them.
- Count, and relate numbers to small quantities.
- Sort objects into groups by size, shape, texture, colour or family.
- Understand the power of 'Yes' and 'No'.
- Work to a simple routine.
- Play with other children – as well as by himself.
- Share toys and play areas.
- Say 'Please,' and 'Thank you,' when appropriate.
- Carry and use handkerchief or tissues.
- Use toilet and handwashing facilities independently.
- Dress and undress without needing help at every stage.
- Respect the property of other people.
- Take out and put away books, games and toys.
- Concentrate on a simple task until it is completed.

Variation in competence in the performance of these tasks will be great, but it is expected that with tutorial assistance and encouragement being available over the whole four year period, progress and achievement will, on average, exceed that currently made. (Here thanks are due to those many parents and infant school teachers who kindly advised on the compilation of these lists).

This section has been dealt with at length because of (i) the importance of the stages to which it refers – birth to four years – and (ii) because it is probably the most radical departure from current practice in this whole teaching-without-schools scheme. The child will be right inside the national education system from birth; he will have trained tutors to help his parents; his parents will have a salary for their full time work with him; he – and his parents – will have recourse to an immense local community resource centre and the benefits of the Central Audio Visual Education Library (CAVEL).

However, although later stages are dealt with more briefly, this is not intended to detract from their importance. Tutors will know that all the compassionate principles listed here for these early stages are applicable equally to all the later stages, i.e. through to middle and later education. But they will know, too, that colleagues who tutor predominantly twelve and thirteen year old pupils will need a special understanding of the needs of children of that age and of the concerns of their parents.

11. Tutor panels

While the personal group of tutor and twenty children will be the basic teaching unit, the tutor panel will be the basic administrative unit of the system. Each personal tutor will be associated with seven colleagues, all of whom will live and practise in the same locality. These eight tutors and their seven groups will form one tutor panel, i.e. seven tutor groups plus one additional tutor who will act, for two years, as tutor panel chairperson. This arrangement can be compared to a panel of general-practice doctors attached to a local health centre.

This arrangement will allow each pupil in the panel to be tutored, for two years at a time, by seven personal tutors: one tutor for each two-year period from birth to fourteen years. These tutors and the chairperson will act as an early-education team of eight professional people. 'Locum' tutors will be registered with each resource centre and will assist during periods of serious illness, maternity leave or other necessary absence.

The tutor panel or team will, with supportive parents, provide for the broad and continuous educational needs of some 140 children i.e. seven groups of twenty pupils. But, in its intimate association with parents and its close relationships with other members of its local community, the panel will be providing educational guidance as it is sought, just as a panel of general practitioners provides guidance for the medical needs of people living in its catchment area. Ultimately the tutor panel will be of greater importance than the medical panel socially, and possibly economically, as its cumulative effects on the community will be far-reaching, ongoing and long-lasting. Indeed one measure of the eventual success of the new tutorial system will be the extent to which tutors reduce the workload of their medical colleagues.

The panel will be largely self-sufficient in terms of teaching skills and the basic subject knowledge needed for helping children in the early-education age groups. Members will have the ability to draw effectively on the huge range of teaching resources available.

Each panel will be self-governing in the administration and financing of its work. It will receive, directly from central government, *per capita* funding for each child registered with it. The distribution of this money on salaries, accommodation and teaching materials will be decided by the tutors themselves.

Parents, with the help of central computerised lists and directories, will choose a tutor for their child's first two-year stage well before the child is born. In this way, they will become associated with the tutor and the panel to which she belongs at the earliest possible stage. During pregnancy parents can be given advice on matters of family-life adjustment, the baby's physical, emotional, social and educational needs from birth, and the preparation required. While medical advice will be given elsewhere, tutoring on child-care in the early months of life can be given before the child is born. This will establish parental relationships with the tutor from the very start of the child's life. Regular contact with a tutor panel will become a normal part of family living.

While there will be no obligation for parent and child to remain with one tutor panel for the whole fourteen years of early education, there will, if all goes well, be many advantages for everyone if there is a long-term association with a single tutor panel.

12. Tutor panel chairpersons

In each tutor panel the additional, or eighth, tutor will, for a period of two years, have no personal group of pupils. Elected for that time by the other tutors in the panel, she will act as chairperson. Following her two years as chairperson she will resume her equally important role as personal tutor to twenty children and be replaced by a newly-elected colleague.

The chairperson's many responsibilities will include giving tutorial help in colleagues' groups as required, helping pupils with particular needs, engaging in research and private study, and tutoring probationer entrants to the new profession. She will consider suggestions for new teaching aids, programmes and courses, whether these are for children, tutors or parents, and with the early trials of those proposals shortlisted for further examination.

With her fellow tutors and with advice from the resource centre warden, she will arrange for the interviewing and appointment of new tutors to the panel.

Another task of the chairperson will be to ensure that a balance of skills is kept within the tutor panel. She will arrange in-service courses, consider carefully new tutorial appointments, and decide whether, as a temporary measure, outside help will be needed. If it is, she will 'buy-in' such help using panel funds. She will also confer with colleagues and parents on any referral of pupils to those consultants available either to the panel or to the community resource centre warden.

Working closely with pupils' parents, each panel will be involved in the preparation of teaching materials and with the reviewing of existing programmes, broadcasts and texts. The chairperson will co-ordinate this work and be responsible for submissions to CAVEL.

While tutors in the panel will specialise in the tutoring of one or two age-groups they will have adequate professional general knowledge of the whole fourteen-year age range. Further, while each tutor will be expected to contribute to the academic, recreational and social objectives of the panel as a whole, she will be able to offer an expertise in several tutoring areas of her own choosing, linked, often, to her university education and her own personal interests. The chairperson will have oversight of this area and ensure that the panel offers its best to local people.

The chairperson will receive no additional salary during her two years in office, but will be paid for extra expenses incurred in this work. This will reinforce the notion that no-one in the new education service will be paid at a higher rate than the professional personal tutor. The chairperson will be on a par with her panel colleagues and will work in partnership with them. In effect she will be taking her turn in administering the panel.

13. Community resource centres

Twelve tutor panels, that is some 96 personal tutors and approximately 1700 pupils aged from birth to fourteen years, will share the educational, social and recreational facilities of a spacious and attractively-designed local community resource centre. Each town or group of villages will have its own resource centre(s) and these will, in the first instance, be adapted from large, unrequired secondary schools. Eventually all centres will be purpose-built. In some cases, according to size, location and the needs of the community, the resource centres will be built on school land, but where school and land are not needed, these will be sold to raise money for new educational projects.

The amount of use that is made of the centres by tutors will vary according to the age of the pupils and the demands of the individual study programmes drawn up for each child. Also, tutors will vary in their approach to their work and this will affect their need for the centres' resources.

The prime function of the resource centre will be to help personal tutors undertake work with their groups. Tutors, in their work, will have first call on the centres' services. These will be provided for eighteen hours a day, from 6 a.m. to midnight, every day throughout the year. Some centres may, at a later stage, remain open for 24 hours and provide a haven for local people at any time.

With such extensive opening, and with such varying degrees of use by tutors, there will be times when the centres will be underused and at these times their facilities will be available to local residents.

Because fixed 'school hours' and fixed 'school terms' as known in the old school-based system will not operate in the new system, there will be periods when groups of pupils or individuals will be studying at or enjoying the recreational facilities of the centres at the same time as older people. This healthy integration of age-groups will replace the isolation felt by teachers in many present-day schools. Such use by the public will be encouraged although it will never be allowed to impinge on the work of pupils and their tutors.

Each resource centre will have a resident warden and deputy warden who will be fully-qualified and experienced tutors. One of their tasks will be to ensure that priority of use is given to tutors and their groups, but a second will be to ensure that the bulk of the facilities are available to the public to the maximum extent possible.

Basic tutoring accommodation at centres will be provided on the assumption that a high proportion of tutoring practice will be done in the homes of pupils and tutors and at other venues. At any one time only a small proportion of the personal groups will be working at the centre so that teaching rooms of the classroom type will not be needed and almost all the former class teaching space of the original secondary schools that are retained initially will be converted to other uses. This very change in accommodation from classroom provision to the supply of small study-areas will both facilitate and stimulate curriculum reform and teaching practice.

Common facilities to be found in all centres will include:

Libraries, laboratories, music rooms, theatre workshops, stages, studios, halls, seminar rooms, private study areas, common and quiet rooms, reading rooms, restaurants, cafes, bars and lounges, sports facilities, gymnasia and swimming pools, tutors' common rooms, grounds and gardens.

For the full-time staff of the centre accommodation will include:

Wardens' study, resource areas for clerical assistants, garages, wardens' flats, caretaker-drivers' houses.

For visitors, particularly visiting tutor groups from other areas, there will be:

Dormitories, housekeeping facilities, tutors' bed-sitting rooms, seminar rooms and offices.

While the accommodation provided will be similar in all centres, it will not be identical. There will be scope for variation to meet local need and to allow tutor panels and wardens to vary their work and to experiment with different groupings, courses and approaches to children's studies.

As, gradually, more and more community-based activities take place in the resource centre, previously-used and less suitable venues can be closed and, where possible, their land and buildings sold. This would save maintenance money for local organisations, provide them with better, permanent facilities, and provide some capital and income to help defray the costs of the newly-built resource centres.

Resource centre staff

As with the accommodation provided, the staffing of the centres will be similar in all cases. There will be some twenty-five employees at each centre and roughly two-thirds of these will work full-time. Use will be made of occasional voluntary help from parents, students, pupils and others, while regular help will be given by older pupils as part of their community service curriculum and by students at the middle and advanced education colleges. In the suggested staffing schedule given below, the number of posts is given in brackets:

Warden (1) and warden-elect (1). Once the new scheme is fully operational, these will be fully-qualified professional personal tutors who have each had at least ten years' tutoring experience. They will have full administrative responsibility for the operation of the centre. Salary will be at the maximum of the tutors' salary scale, with free residential accommodation provided at the centre. If they wish, wardens can let their own homes for their period in office, perhaps on lease to other education service personnel, with insurance and legal fees paid from resource centre funds.

Both wardens will assist with the administration of those twelve tutor panels in the area which are attached to the resource centre. Wardens will be available in an advisory capacity to help parents, especially with their first and, perhaps, subsequent choices of tutors and tutor panels. The wardens will assist by working in a tutor panel as time allows and, when such help is agreed with personal tutors, in a personal group. They will value these opportunities to renew their tutoring skills. Other duties will include visiting resource centres in other areas, organising conferences and courses, and the entertainment of overseas delegates.

Each warden will hold office for four years; two as warden-elect followed by two as warden. Both post holders will be elected from and by the personal tutors of the twelve panels attached to the centre. After their four-year terms of office they will resume their work as personal tutors in their panels.

Specialist staff (5). There will be specialist tutoring staff attached to the centre whose work will be to aid personal tutors with teaching in areas such as physical education, games and swimming, drama, arts and crafts. They will be responsible for the supervision and organisation of these activities and for meeting all associated legal requirements. All will be experienced teachers or coaches in their fields and will be paid at a rate similar to personal tutors. Also, they will, as available, conduct classes timetabled for the general public.

Librarians (4). The librarian and a qualified assistant will administer all aspects of the resource centre's libraries and will work with tutors, their pupils and the general public. There will be two ancillary library assistants, and help in the libraries will also be given by older pupils from tutor panels and by students

Figure 6. Community resource centre facilities and plan.

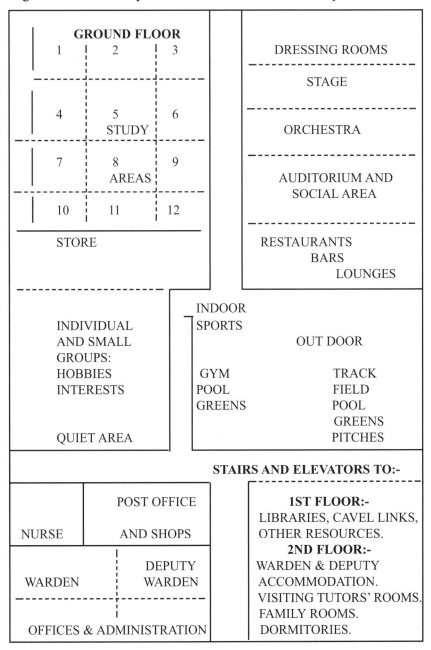

from middle and advanced-education colleges. The librarian will be allocated funds from panel chairpersons for resource purchases and will consult with tutors about their library needs. Librarians will make use of the inter-loan network between centre libraries and the Internet. The librarian will be paid a tutor's salary, and will help with the tutoring of older pupils interested in library work.

Bursar (1). The bursar will be responsible to the warden for the finances of the centre and its associated tutor panels, and will employ and supervise the work of clerical staff.

Secretaries (2). One secretary will be full-time and an assistant secretary will be employed part-time. They will assist the wardens, bursar and tutors as required.

Some secretarial work will be done by students from advanced-education colleges as part of their course.

Technicians (2). Two technicians will help the librarian and edit and catalogue audio-visual material for use by tutors and will maintain equipment. They will be conversant with the transmissions from the Central Audio-Visual Education Library (CAVEL) and with the reception of its material at the centre and at those places of work chosen by personal tutors. They will advise on technical aspects of programme-making by tutors and tutor groups.

Caretaker-drivers (2). In addition to usual caretaking duties, these workers will drive and maintain the centre's transport, including the minibuses used by tutors for educational visits. As the centre will be open daily for the whole year, the caretaker-drivers will live on-site and employ part-time assistants as agreed with the warden.

Domestic staff (7). There will be employment for a groundsman, a chef and restaurant workers, housekeeper, cleaners and launderers, both full-time and part-time. They will be helped by older pupils as part of their community service, and by college students interested in such work as a possible career.

Nurses (2). Eventually the local health centre will be situated on the same campus as the resource centre. Two of the nurses at the health centre will have responsibility for the healthcare of staff, tutors and children associated with the resource centre. The aid of a nurse will be to hand whenever the centre is open and both nurses will help with teaching children about health matters including personal hygiene and personal relationships.

Excluding the nurses, who will be paid from health centre funds, each resource centre will have some twenty-five support staff whose first responsibility will be to help personal tutors in their work. Some, occasionally, and with prior personal tutor approval, will help directly with the instruction of pupils in specific skills, or give guidance to tutors wishing to undertake some specialised teaching themselves. Their second duty will be to assist in the running of the

Figure 7. Community resource centre staff.

Position	No	Tenure	Hours	Appointment
Warden	1	2 years	Full-time	Elected by tutors
Warden-elect	1	2 years	Full-time	Elected by tutors
Specialist staff	5	Permanent	*(see note 1)**	Appointed by warden
Librarian	1	Permanent	Full-time	Appointed by warden
Assistant librarian	1	Permanent	Full-time	Appointed by warden
Ancillary librarians	2	Temporary	Full-time*	Appointed by librarian
Bursar	1	Permanent	Full-time	Appointed by warden
Secretary	1	Permanent	Full-time	Appointed by bursar
Assistant Secretary	1	Temporary	Part-time	Appointed by bursar
Technicians	2	Permanent	Full-time*	Appointed by warden and CAVEL
Caretaker-drivers	2	Permanent	Full-time*	Appointed by bursar
Chef	1	Permanent	Full-time	Appointed by bursar
Assistant Chef	1	Temporary	Full-time	Appointed by bursar
Housekeeper	1	Permanent	Full-time	Appointed by bursar
Asst. domestic staff	3	Temporary	Full-time*	Appointed by housekeeper
Groundsman	1	Permanent	Full-time	Appointed by bursar
Nurses	(2)	*See note 2*	*See note 2*	Employed by RHA

*or part time equivalent. *Note 1:* may be employed full-time for length of particular courses, and be part-time equivalent. *Note 2:* employed by regional health authority and seconded to community resource centre.

centre for the benefit of the local community, of which they themselves will be important members.

As part of their work in the community-service elements of the curriculum, and at an age considered appropriate by parents and tutors, pupils will undertake regular duties at their resource centre. In a practical way this work will help to reinforce aspects of each pupil's emerging social philosophy, i.e. the need for each member of the community to make a contribution to its wellbeing. Regular help in the cleaning, decoration, general repair and ground maintenance of the centre will be an integral part of the pupil's social development and an important factor in containing management costs in the running of the centre.

The administrative arrangements for this work, including the compilation of rosters, will be made by support staff, not by tutors. But always tutors will be required to suggest and approve such work in any pupil's study programme. Pupils' work in this area, approximately from the age of eight, will be assessed and such assessment will be included in reports made on pupils' progress.

With so many varying facilities open to children and their tutors, and with these facilities and others open to people living locally, the social value of the resource centre to the community it serves will be immense.

The value of this provision is being recognised by governments: e.g. in the British government's green paper of December 1998. But what is envisaged in this book, *Teaching Tomorrow*, is much more ambitious and far-reaching: it makes the community resource centres and field centres central to the new approach to the whole of a community's educational opportunities, as did Henry Morris's architecturally-fashioned village colleges in Cambridgeshire many years ago..

14. Field centres

A country-wide network of small schools will be retained to provide field centres for use in the new education system. These centres will provide day and boarding facilities sufficient for two or three personal groups plus accommodation for accompanying tutors and some parents. (See Figure 8, page 95).

Centres will be in all regions and in urban and rural localities. Some, for general studies, will be in areas of outstanding natural beauty, others in interesting towns, and others sited for special study work as in history, geography, and the general and social sciences or the settings of carefully chosen novels.

All centres, at all times, will be available solely for leisure purposes and will give all children over the age of eight the opportunity to enjoy simple, interesting holidays with other children, parents or other family members, and personal tutors. Again, stress will be laid on the many-faceted nature of learning.

Accommodation will be basic with dormitory accommodation for up to twenty boys and twenty girls. There will be equally simple but separate arrangements for parents and tutors. Dining rooms, recreational rooms, a library which will be strong on local publications and materials, a map room, a meeting or seminar room and private study areas, will be basic to all field centres.

Each centre will have a resident warden who will be a qualified and experienced personal tutor who has specialised knowledge of her centre's locality. She will lead field trips, give talks, set assignments, assist tutors and parents to take advantage of the area's resources, and maintain and administer the centre – particularly its library. She will have the assistance throughout the year of small groups of student-tutors in training – possibly three or four at a time. Often these students will be from other countries where a teaching-without-schools scheme is in operation. She will be paid at the same rate as a personal tutor but will have accommodation and board provided in return for residential duties and the supervision of student-tutors.

While the field centre warden's position will be a permanent one, she will be required, as part of her ongoing in-service professional training, to assist a tutor panel with its normal work. For that time her place at the field centre will be filled by a personal tutor interested in the possibility of taking up field centre work later in her career, and she too will be assisted by student tutors in training.

It will be important to retain sufficient smaller strategically-placed school buildings to provide these amenities nationwide. They will be available to all groups whether the tutor wishes to embark on a one-day visit or to set up a week-long study period. This will need to be decided at the outset of the new teaching-children-without schools scheme so that suitable schools and their land are not sold off and lost in the early years.

Many small railway stations and branch lines could have been retained in the 1950s and 1960s for similar purposes and to provide a nationwide network of trails for pedestrians and cyclists, but the opportunity was lost and will never be regained. This lack of foresight must be avoided when large numbers of schools are closed during the 21st century.

The field centres will be open year-round. Experiencing seasonal weather in different parts of the country will be part of the learning programme. Children will be offered the opportunity to see different aspects of existing industries and view remnants of those long gone. They will see, as will their parents and tutors, regions of their own or other countries not normally visited by tourists. They will be able to study these regions with the expert help of wardens, their assistants and the multimedia. At the same time, for older pupils, local studies of this nature will be built into their personal programmes of work and earn them credit. All field centres will be able to receive up-to-the-minute data on their localities from CAVEL in the normal way, and CAVEL will provide similar information services to tutors working in other countries at any time and in any language required.

Sufficient provision must be made for groups of older children and students from other nations to be accommodated in field centres so that they can take part in wide-ranging programmes of international visits and exchanges.

As there will be no 'school year' or 'school term' as in the old school-based system, a pupil's total of eighteen years in early, middle and advanced education will be measured in calendar years and months. Within this time there will be set an initial target of two weeks per calendar year for studying or relaxing at a field centre for all pupils in each of their last two years of early education. A week of this might be made up of several one-or two-day sessions. Younger children, from age six, will begin with day visits, and then distance and length of time away from home will be gradually extended. Parents who accompany groups will be asked to pay their own expenses for the use of the centre on an 'at cost' basis. When available, field centres will be open to the general public for holidays and short breaks again for an 'at-cost' payment. Reservations for tutor groups will be made through CAVEL, and for parents through their local community resource centre.

The benefits will be many:

● Children will visit, at length, other regions of their country as part of their educational programme under qualified supervision and tuition.

● They, and those parents who accompany them, will gain socially from the experience.

● The notion that 'education lies everywhere all the time' will be demonstrated and strengthened.

● There will be many chances for tutors and parents to exchange views and to get to know each other and the children better than can be achieved in a more formal school-based system.

● Children – and some parents – will be introduced to areas that might interest them for the rest of their lives and provide them with holiday destinations for many years to come.

● As other countries develop a similar system of nation-wide field centres, exchanges for older children and for students in later-education schemes and student-tutors will be simply and economically available and will further the idea of everyone having to live peacefully in one finite world.

As part of the young person's social and academic development, and as an instrument of further understanding between children, parents and their tutors, field centres will be an essential element in the teaching-without-schools format. The centres' position in the network of venues available for tutors' use is shown in Figure 9 (page 98): *Venues available for study.*

Figure 8. Field centre facilities and plan.

1	2	3	4	PATIO
STUDY AREAS				PICNIC
5	6	7	8	AREAS
9	10	11	12	→

LIBRARY

CAVEL LINKS

MAP ROOMS

TEACHING AND SEMINARS

RECREATIONAL AREA

(DAY AND BOARDING)

FILM AND VIDEO

RESIDENTIAL AREAS
(Ground and first floors)

DORMITORIES
LAUNDRY
DRYING ROOMS

DINING

AREAS

CAFETERIA

KITCHENS

POST OFFICE AND
SHOPS

| MEDICAL CENTRE | OFFICES & STORES | STUDENT TUTORS | WARDEN |
| OFFICES & ADMINISTRATION | | RECEPTION | |

95

15. Central Audio-Visual Education Library (CAVEL)

Each pupil's individual study programme will be an essential feature of the new system. The compilation of the programme will depend partly on the ready availability to each tutor of thousands of pre-recorded, accurately-described, annotated and graded audio-visual clips, lessons, programmes or units. These will be made ready for transmission at any time to any venue chosen by a personal tutor for her group or for individual pupils and parents. Material will also be available from, and can be transmitted to, audio-visual education libraries abroad. It will be additional to, but separate from, Internet data.

Transmission will be from a Central Audio-Visual Education Library (CAVEL). The library's stock, meticulously indexed and cross-referenced, will be supplemented by explanatory notes. It will have source lists and printed supplementary text as well as material for testing, assessment and revision. For very young children the experiences offered will be wholly enjoyable, and, for most pupils, will only gradually take on a more formal aspect as they near the end of their early education years.

With much of her basic, routine preparatory work done for her, a key function of the tutor will be the consolidation of trusting personal relationships with each pupil and parent. This will be a vital part of the new role as tutors are relieved of school duties and so are able to give even more of their time to the establishment of sound working relationships with pupils and colleagues.

In this the tutor will be aided by the need to compile, with families, study programmes for children in her personal group. She will bring into play here her knowledge of her pupil, parents' abilities and interests, home-study facilities, and her own skills in matching these to a programme of expertly-formulated lesson units available through CAVEL to her pupil, his parents and herself, and from facilities offered at the community resource centre and at field centres. Because of the need for consultation, she will be in direct contact with child and parent and have, as a starting point, something important to discuss. There should be no awkward silences.

Material will be available from the Central Audio-Visual Education Library (CAVEL) which library will itself be conveniently situated in a mid county or state and, in order to facilitate staff exchanges and visits from at home and abroad, close to the rail and motorway network and an international airport. CAVEL will contain meeting rooms, accommodation and catering facilities for many visiting tutors, recreational areas, study accommodation and fully-equipped studios and libraries for the making of educational programmes.

The library will be set in pleasant grounds similar to those of an attractive university campus. Its huge car-parking areas will be needed by the 25% of the nation's tutors who will visit it routinely each year.

Any lesson units stocked by CAVEL will be immediately available at any pupil's or tutor's home on a tv or radio receiver at any time throughout the year. Because of this, parents will be able to follow or take part in any child's study programme. No copyright will exist in programmes; they will be public property to be paid for and used by the public.

Curriculum areas

CAVEL lesson stock will be in one of five categories, each of which corresponds to a major curriculum area (see pages 66 to 71). These will be:

(i) literacy and numeracy
(ii) combined studies and/or general knowledge
(iii) the arts
(iv) leisure and recreation
(v) local community, national and international service and, listed here in order
    to match the six areas listed on page 65:
(vi) social philosophy – including international understanding.

– although this sixth category will not be presented as a CAVEL category since it will not be regarded as a separate or individual subject for particular teaching purposes. It will be an area primarily concerned with the child's emerging social conscience and will be regarded as a ubiquitous and integral part of the entire curriculum span. It will be developed gradually and incidentally through work undertaken in the five other areas. Few audio-visual programmes alone are likely to succeed directly in inculcating healthy, positive social attitudes in children. Indeed, with certain children at certain ages, the opposite is likely to occur. It is in this sixth category that the work of the skilled personal tutor will be essential and of great value. It will be the one area, above all others, where her work can never be replaced, even by the most sophisticated technology. Her successful work here will add greatly to her professionalism.

Lessons or units in the other curriculum areas will be of immense help if those social values are implicit in the programmes' material and if the presence of those values can be relied upon by parent and tutor. Much of the excellent work currently undertaken by teachers who use carefully-chosen books, especially in English and other literature, can in future be augmented *but not replaced* by means of the audio-visual media. Programme units will be produced by CAVEL personnel with this morally supportive role in mind.

In each of the five areas, material will be categorised to assist parents and tutors in their initial choices. Singly or together parents and tutors will be able to preview material and assess its value for individual pupils.

Programme or lesson material in each curriculum area will be divided into seven bands or levels of difficulty, each one corresponding approximately to one of the seven stages of early education. However, these suggested levels can be

Figure 9. Venues available for study.

Family home:

Study area
Book corner
Computer room
CAVEL link
Garden

Tutor's home:

Study
Library
Tutor-panel link
CAVEL link

Community resource centre:

Study areas   Seminar rooms
Libraries   CAVEL link
Art, craft, music rooms and studios
Hall, stage, auditorium
Quiet rooms, reading rooms
Tutorial rooms
Sports facilities: pool, track, field, gymnasium

Local venues:

Museums
Art galleries
Churches
Theatres
Cinemas
Libraries
Factories
Shops
Hotels
Parks
Leisure centres
Youth centres
Stations
Airports
Colleges

Distant venues:
- home and abroad

Heritage centres:
- Houses
- Gardens
- Castles
Cathedrals
Forests
Farms
National parks
Railways
Canals
Arboreta
Youth hostels
Craft centres
Nature trails
Rivers
Radio/tv studios
Mountains

Field centre:

Day and boarding.
National/international network of centres based on disused schools in rural and urban areas with study facilities -
library, CAVEL link.

Colleges/Universities:

Study, library, seminar facilities available during vacations with reciprocal arrangements with institutions abroad.

Outdoor venues

Parks, recreation grounds, leisure centres, pools, professional and amateur sports clubs.

Other:

Additional venues known to and chosen by tutors and families.

98

waived entirely if the tutor thinks the level is inappropriate for those of her pupils whose ability and stage of development require the use of material from a higher or lower band. The bands will be for guidance only.

CAVEL material will be further categorised into that which is aimed at pupils and that aimed at parents and tutors. A third category will be principally for tutors and will offer alternative approaches, ideas for follow-up work and pupil involvement and the assessment – by pupil, parent or tutor (or all three) – of work already done.

Pupils' programmes will contain basic lesson material; information, examples, illustrations, references, dramatisations, film episodes and details of work to be completed.

Programmes for parents and tutors will contain examples of earlier work done on that material by other pupils of varying ages and abilities, recent comment made on the lesson by tutor panels, evaluations of it, proposed amendments, alternative ways in which the material might be used with different students, lists of other appropriate lessons or material, books and films of value in continuing or varying an approach to the topic, names of local tutors or parents who have used the material already or those who have a special interest in that topic area.

A further subdivision of material will be between that intended for (i) initial learning i.e. material likely to be new to the pupil, and (ii) that intended for revision, and (iii) that intended for tutor or parent assessment of a pupil's work, or for pupil self-assessment. Where further work on a topic is suggested the coding for an alternative or supplementary unit will be given.

Older pupils will learn the mechanics of the coding system for identifying material from CAVEL and will be able to call up their own lesson units according to how their needs are indicated by their personal study programme and their tutor. They will be able to repeat units or parts of units or take supplementary and alternative lessons and then undertake follow-up work making use of some of the activities suggested. They will be able to test themselves enjoyably, record progress accurately, and move on promptly to new work.

They will be able to work singly or in small groups. They will follow up points taken from the lessons in tutorials with their personal tutor or with another tutor who is asked to help them temporarily because of her specialist knowledge.

Although the initial establishment of CAVEL will be expensive, the cost will be justified long-term because the excellent material prepared and stored will be used many times and will be available to thousands of parents and tutors and to even more pupils if and when they need it. Each will be of a quality that a teacher working on her own – producing her own material – could not match.

Most programmes will be current for several years while others will need

Figure 10. The Central Audio-Visual Education Library (CAVEL).

Basements — — — — — — — — — Stock/Filing/Administration (Library stock)					

Ground floor Lobby	A	B	C	D	E
Reception		Five studios			
Offices					

	1	2	3	4
	Eight seminar rooms			
Editorial work areas	5	6	7	8

Theatre A	1		Four libraries:
	2 small		
	3 viewing		1. Basement (stock)
	4 rooms		2. Ground floor
Theatre B	5		3. First floor
	6		4. Second floor
Theatre C	7		

Production work-area	Transmission facilities

First floor:
Library, Recreation – dining – bars

Second floor:
Library, Accommodation   Residents
                                            Visitors

100

frequent updating or replacement. While likely length of life will be a factor considered in the making of lesson units by tutor-producers at the outset, it will not be a highly significant one.

There will be dangers in too heavy a reliance on centrally-produced, stored and distributed lesson units and these will need to be recognised and countered. Similarly, expectations must not be raised unreasonably by extravagant claims. Often, in the past, the latest idea or trend in education that has found favour with the establishment has been hailed as the 'final answer' or 'ultimate solution' to pupils', teachers' and schools' problems. Quite obvious difficulties in implementation and practice have been ignored, as have some of the consequences that might follow the continuation of those policies. Sometimes the mildest of objectors have been labelled 'reactionary' when all they have been trying to do is raise doubts about the possible effects of the proposals or indicate immediate drawbacks or likely long-term problems. Their objections have been swept aside as the bandwagon rolled relentlessly on collecting careerists by the dozen.

This intolerance of well-intentioned questioning has hastened the growth of teacher cynicism. Much has been lost because claims made for a new approach or method or organisation have been unrealistic. The same ideas could have brought greater benefits if the difficulties and disadvantages had been recognised with frankness at the outset. The introduction of mixed-ability grouping and teaching to primary schools and later to secondary schools, across all subjects, perhaps serves as an example. However, in this proposal, to teach-children-without-schools, the dangers as well as the benefits of heavy usage of the new information technology will be acknowledged and taken into account.

A distinct advantage will be the high quality of the lesson units prepared for tutors' consideration and possible use. The study of some current domestic television natural history programmes will quickly indicate qualities of illustration, demonstration, elucidation, conciseness and fascination that are far beyond the production capacity of even the most gifted teacher. That significant gap is likely to widen as media technology improves and as the difficulties faced by teachers in schools increase. Instead of being used largely as supplementary material within an existing curriculum, multimedia programmes will form the *basis* of the syllabus, and the programmes themselves will be entirely within the public domain for the use of all at any time.

A painstakingly-produced professional reading of an extract from a novel, or presentation of a scene from a play, will enhance the study of both book and drama. Through the resources of CAVEL an immense range of readings, the dramatisation of thousands of books and productions of hundreds of plays will be available at precisely the time and ability level that the parent or tutor wishes it to appear in the child's individual study programme. As many repeats as are needed will be no problem, and homing in on a particular paragraph, speech or verse will be instantaneous. All will aid, but not replace, the pupil's reading of the novel or his attendance at, or performance in, a production of the play.

Precise explanations of points in mathematics and the sciences made on screen and supported in print will often be clearer to the pupil than either the teacher's or the textbook writer's explanations can hope to be. But in practice, with individual tuition made possible, each teaching mode will assist the other.

Such interaction and mutual support will be vital. Technology, no matter how refined it becomes, will not replace the tutor. Only the tutor, working with the parent, will know fully, at first hand, the individual child's needs and be able to address them at the necessary personal level. The technology will be seen first as a liberator because it will free teachers from the restrictions of the school-based system, then as an enhancer, for it will add greatly to teachers' potency as true educators and the children's enjoyment as willing learners.

These advantages will increase as tutors become skilled in the use of the lesson-units and supplementary material and as they appreciate fully their range and effectiveness. Some tutors will become producers of programmes and will use their talents and professionalism to ensure that the programmes made are wholly pupil-tutor orientated. With knowledgeable, critical tutors working with groups of pupils submitting regular user-reports to CAVEL, programmes will be under constant scrutiny. They will be amended immediately if there is wide-spread objection as to suitability or, if there is less urgency, at the scheduled two-yearly review of material. Accepted criticisms and suggestions originating from tutors' reports will be built into tutors' programmes or the accompanying commentary or notes.

In this way tutors will realise that the CAVEL output is under the surveillance of practising tutors like themselves. While, within CAVEL programmes, they will be using basic material prepared by others, they will, by virtue of their own submissions to CAVEL, be more intimately engaged in the origination, production and revision of teaching material than were many teachers who worked in the old school-based system. Tutors who so choose will have opportunities to influence what is produced and presented and the ways in which that is done.

As they preview and select particular 'lessons' study units or series, tutors will think of different ways of using them with their own pupils. At the same time they will know that all lessons will be available when and where they are needed. This reliable availability will increase tutors' confidence in the CAVEL material and encourage them to build appropriate sections into their work. They will be less dependent on their own time-limited ability to provide resources. They will be working with and adapting to their pupils' needs teaching material which many tutors have worked in partnership first to create and, later, to amend and adapt.

The school-based situation will be avoided in which the teacher is unable to defend either the relevance or the quality of what is being offered to pupils apart from the possibility that it might be of use in helping children pass tests and examinations at some time in the future. Even this defence is weakened by the knowledge that the bulk of what is learned in this way will be forgotten quickly once the test has been taken and passed.

So, as things stand, many schoolteachers, unsure of the value of what they are doing, and conscious of what they *could* be doing, take on a defensive attitude in dealings with their pupils and under such circumstances work-induced stress will grow. At times the stress will become too much and, not surprisingly, some teachers will break down altogether. To require teachers to deliver lessons of doubtful value to classes of children already sceptical of school and difficult to control is demanding too much.

Also avoided will be the position in which school-based pupils are required to study set topics or set books in specified rooms for predetermined times. Those constants will have been decided months beforehand by others in order to meet the needs of a fixed venue, a fixed syllabus and a fixed timetable in a firmly fixed school term, semester or year.

Such forward planning by those who have no immediate contact with the consequences of what they have decreed is not desirable as it cannot possibly be based on the personal needs of pupils and teachers. The planners cannot know what these needs are likely to be so far ahead, and the least sensitive of them will be largely unaware of many of these needs and predilections anyway.

There are, for instance, times when people, young and old, do not wish to read a novel, view a film, listen to music, write a story, ponder a mathematical conundrum, play netball, bake a cake, and so on. These highly personal and fluctuating disinclinations arise for varied reasons some of which will be inexplicable and very few of which need be reprehensible.

To stipulate that *The Merchant of Venice* (Act I, scene iii) will be read by thirty-four pupils between 9.25 a.m. and 10.10 a.m. on Tuesdays in the geography room because that is when and where literature has been slotted into the class's timetable, or that twenty-nine girls should enjoy gymnastics for forty minutes in the middle of Thursday afternoons for the same administratively-dictated reasons may, for many children, be doing more harm than good. This is inexcusable both in altruistic terms and in economic terms for these lessons are costing the taxpayer a great deal of money day by day throughout the year for negative returns. The nation is paying handsomely for nothing, while the pupil is gaining disrespect for the whole concept of education.

But the embracing of a system offering small personal tutor groups in a non-school, non-regimented learning environment with the use of individual study programmes made possible by tutors' professional skills in the use of CAVEL's technology, range and flexibility will remove the timetable straitjacket. The only timetables in use will be those compiled by the tutor for the benefit of her pupils, their parents and herself.

In many ways the necessarily restrictive school-based system is, and has been for a long time, an obstacle to enjoyable, long-lasting learning. The movement from century-old schools, which is now an option, will permit childhood education to become a more humane and effective process. Some of our older universities have known the value of a tutorial system for a very long time: now that system can be made available to the many rather than the few.

Under teaching-without-schools, minimum time will be spent on the acquisition of the textbook type knowledge that can readily be obtained, as needed, from a variety of sources: printed or electronic. To the fore will be a consideration of the meaning of the child's life and the many relationships that life gives rise to, rather than the learning of easily-obtained facts about the world in which that life is lived.

Such a new approach will provide unlimited scope for the capable and imaginative tutor, and her work will be immensely satisfying. But, conversely, failure to provide absorbing, informative and enjoyable study programmes will be largely of her own making. The well-worn excuses offered by weaker teachers for their pupils' low level of interest and achievement and their own low level of work satisfaction will no longer hold good. The faults and remedies will lie mainly with the tutors.

The prodigious range of audio-visual lesson units available from CAVEL and from programmes in the tutor's own stock, combined with reliable, ever-ready equipment, will enable several pupils to take different, self-selected lessons during the same study period. The personal tutor will have the ability to propose to parent and child not only what material should be selected, but where, when and how it should be studied. Additionally, the tutor will be able to work alongside one pupil or several and discuss, encourage, elaborate, question and assess as she thinks fit. In other words she will be enabled to practise as a fully-fledged professional person making her own choices at her own venue in her own way to her own timing and all for the benefit of her client.

All lesson units will be available for public reception. Comments will be sought and CAVEL tutorial and production staff will be required to respond. Parents will have copies of their children's study programmes and will be able to view, at any time, with or without their children, those units being studied. They will become as deeply involved in the children's work as they themselves choose to be.

A selection of supplementary material will be supplied by CAVEL and will be stocked at community resource centres where it will be available to all. At the resource centres and field centres parents, as part of their contract, (page 141) will be encouraged to discuss material, formally and informally, with other parents and with other tutors. This occasional discussion will be uninhibited and, because of this, informative to tutors and resource centre staff alike. Significant comments will be forwarded to CAVEL for examination and specific responses will be required from CAVEL-based tutors.

Safeguards

Resource centre wardens, with tutor panel chairpersons, will arrange seminars for tutors at which audio-visual teaching material will be evaluated. Opinion will be given on lesson quality, the value of follow-up work done or envisaged, and pupil-parent reaction to material already used. Regular, scheduled seminars will be held for parents and others at community resource centres at which comments will be heard, ideas assessed and future programmes discussed. This ongoing public awareness and involvement will be an important safeguard. But these sessions will be an opportunity for parents to raise, in a seemingly incidental way, other matters of concern which they would like to talk through. A sensitive, perceptive tutor will realise that, although these raised concerns are not of immediate relevance to the CAVEL programme under review, they are important to one or more parents present and that their concerns are, at that moment, more urgent than the review of the lesson unit. She will help a discussion to develop so that the problem can be aired fully. Later she may wish to report to CAVEL, through her panel chairperson, the need to allow for such items to be included when programmes are reconsidered.

During their professional training, personal tutors will be made aware of the need for safeguards. They will learn how to use critically and imaginatively many lessons emanating from a single source. Emphasis will be put on the need for tutors to make use of their own, their pupils' and their pupils' parents' varying personal interpretations of lessons. These will be based, partly, on their own viewpoint, expertise and experience. They will consider ways of encouraging children to appraise material for themselves even if, at times, this discussion has to be tutor-initiated or sustained. They will consider ways in which individual or small-group activities can be devised and varied, and these exchanges will, in themselves, act as an antidote to unwanted uniformity.

As an essential requirement for professional qualification, tutors will have to show that they are conversant with the whole range of material stored at CAVEL. The stock will be great and cover many approaches and viewpoints. It will be possible for tutors to construct well-balanced individual study programmes provided they are thoroughly conversant with CAVEL's range of lesson material and keep abreast of changes made to it. Tutors will be taught that this new expertise, i.e. knowledge of the material available to them, will largely replace the subject-based or general knowledge expected of their school-based predecessors.

Also during training, student-tutors will be helped to understand how they and their future clients can make best use of the less obvious potential of CAVEL material. They will realise that lesson units will rarely be used in exactly the same way by any two tutors or pupils, and that some approaches and interpretations will emerge which were not envisaged by the programme's tutor-producers. This will be further protection against a widespread uniformity of teaching and learning.

Qualified tutors and student-tutors will be expected to offer their own ideas and material for new lesson series. They will advise at various stages of preparation, and will review the units after production.

Ongoing tutor involvement in CAVEL's work will add to professional satisfaction and development, and will ensure that small groups of tutor-producers at CAVEL do not acquire unacceptable levels of influence on what is taught. For no one will 'a job at CAVEL' become a sinecure or an easy alternative to the difficult and demanding work of personal tutoring.

Further safeguards will be the regular replacement of CAVEL staff after clearly-stipulated periods of duty. There will be the presence at the library of temporarily-attached tutors drawn from those panel chairpersons who choose to undertake that work and who accept training and show competence and flair. Another major shield will be the daily involvement of tutors and parents in the monitoring of lesson units transmitted to them in the course of their work. Personal tutors will never be regarded as passive receivers and users of other tutors' lesson material.

Again, once the teaching-without-schools scheme is fully operational, permanent production staff at CAVEL will be first and foremost qualified and widely-experienced personal tutors. Once appointed, each staff member will be seconded every eight years to practise, for two years, in a tutor panel. There will be no exceptions to this even for the most gifted producer. Nor will there be deviation from the rule that no person in the education service will be paid more than the fully experienced personal tutor. There will be many rewards in CAVEL work, but, apart from additional expenses legitimately claimed, they will never be pecuniary.

The library will be governed by an independent council of twenty-one people. This CAVEL council will appoint and dismiss staff and monitor the use of funds. It will be able to reject lesson units or demand amendments but, normally, will use this power only when it is demonstrated that there has been widespread or prolonged or serious complaint.

The council will consist of twenty-one members, three being elected from each of seven bodies:

● CAVEL permanent staff: all professionally-qualified tutors.

- The Professional Tutors' Guild: all professionally-qualified tutors.
- Resource centre wardens: all professionally-qualified tutors.
- Tutor panel chairpersons: all professionally-qualified tutors.
- Parents' associations.
- Central government.
- Local government.

This composition of the council will ensure that a majority of members is drawn from the tutoring profession.

The two principal items in the charter establishing CAVEL and governing its work will be that (i) the library's production of audio-visual lesson-units and supporting materials must always be aimed at the social and educational needs of children from their birth to age fourteen and that (ii) such materials must be free of political or religious bias and free of material likely to corrupt or distress children.

The council and CAVEL staff will see their role as one of quietly supporting personal tutors and parents in their work, and never as one of replacing them.

Each year CAVEL editorial staff will publish a pamphlet for distribution to all households outlining the facilities offered by the library, its staffing and operational arrangements, and the opportunities available for public visiting and inspection.

Also published will be a comprehensive annual library handbook which will give interested parties much more detail on its work and government. Also included will be technological data covering origin, production, transmission and storing of lesson units, and information on reference facilities and the means of accessing them.

Such a Central Audio-Visual Education Library is no mere pipe dream. Given the initial large outlay of money, the library and its work are quite feasible and there are clear and encouraging signs that the British Government appreciates some of the exciting possibilities offered. (Green Paper, December 1998). The Internet gives already – in 1999 – an idea of what could, with careful, professional tutorial help, be offered to children on an enjoyable, regular, day-to-day basis. They would be learning in a new world.

16. Brochures

Each tutor panel, resource centre and field centre will publish and regularly revise, its own brochure detailing its staff, structure and work. See Figure 11: *The publication and content of brochures,* (page 110).

Tutor panel brochures
Tutor panel brochures will be revised every two years by the outgoing chair-

person in consultation with the new incumbent. The brochure will be in seven sections. It will be freely available to parents.

Careful comparison of brochures will assist parents in placing their children, and will help tutors who wish to apply for membership of a particular panel.

For their adequate recruitment of pupils, panels will rely on a reputation for concerned tutoring, excellent professional relationships with parents and pupils, and the quality of the individual study programmes they devise. These points must be covered strongly in the panel's brochure in order to assist pupil recruitment.

No funds will be available to a panel which consistently fails to recruit and retain pupils, but the Professional Tutors' Guild (PTG) will advise such panels before recruitment falls to a dangerously low level. When requested, the PTG will ask a team of experienced, successful tutors to make recommendations for improvement or to offer help with brochure-writing and distribution.

The brochure's seven sections will be:

1. Tutors' professional qualifications, interests, tutoring experience, age-groups preferred for tutoring.

2. A statement, written by each tutor, of her aims in her work, her priorities and her specialisms.

3. A schedule of times when each tutor is available to talk about her pupils' progress. These times will be in addition to the many informal discussions that will arise naturally during each two-year stage. The more formal, scheduled consultations will be arranged through the community resource centre's clerical staff and these will take place in the tutor's or child's home or in study rooms set aside for the purpose in the resource centre.

Although relationships between tutors and parents will be informal and friendly, the publication in the brochure of such a schedule will ensure that all tutors will be available to their clients professionally, at specified times, in a manner that equates with the practices of lawyers, doctors, dentists, veterinary surgeons and other professionals.

The sometimes less than satisfactory 'parents' evenings' of the school-based system, which can be hurried, crowded and lacking in privacy, will disappear with few tears shed.

Also published in the brochure will be details of the emergency 'on-call' tutor who will be available to help anxious parents or older pupils when required at awkward, unscheduled times. The panel chairperson will maintain the 'on-call' roster and include herself on it. The chairperson will be responsible for publishing occasional newsletters to parents and others and these will include details of the 'on-call' roster.

4. Extracts will be given from each of seven individual study programmes compiled during the previous two years for pupils in the seven age groups within the

panel. These extracts will give an insight to work done and the standards sought. Often they will be the basis of discussion at exploratory meetings when parents are considering panel choice.

5. The brochure will show how the staffing and work of the panel fits into the nation's wider education system, particularly demonstrating how it is linked to the next two stages covered by the middle and advanced education colleges. It will indicate 'normal' or 'average' levels of language development and numeracy in a child at the centre-point of each of the seven stages. This, too, will be helpful to parents unsure of the best way to discuss progress with their child's personal tutor or uncertain as to whether their child is developing within the normally accepted 'satisfactory' range of differences.

6. There will be a listing of the uses made of the facilities available at the community resource centre and the part parents can play, and, similarly, of uses made of field centres. Reference will be made to links with resource centres and field centres abroad, to the facilities available, and to ways in which families can be helped to make best use of them.

7. The Agreed National Code covering the rights and responsibilities of all using the education service will be reproduced, with notes, at the end of each brochure. This Agreed National Code (ANC) is set out on pages 141 to 145.

Resource centre brochures

Resource centre brochures will be revised annually. Stress will be laid on the facilities available to the general public. Publication and distribution will be the responsibility of the resource centre warden. In the brochure she will give:

● Professional details of centre staff as in tutor panel brochures.

● An account of the part played by the centre in the work of personal groups and the facilities they are offered.

● Details of the facilities open to the general public and the times these are most likely to be available.

● Assurance that the centre is run for the benefit of the whole community; particular mention will be made of libraries, reading rooms, study rooms, music and drama facilities, sports provision, restaurants and lounges.

● A list of ways in which volunteers can help in the centre.

● A list of which facilities are free of charge and which attract an 'at cost' charge for those able to pay and of concessions available for those who cannot.

● Information about resource centres abroad, including details of residential study courses and student and family exchange schemes.

Field centre brochures

Similarly, field centre wardens will publish a brochure relevant to their centre,

Figure 11. The publication and content of brochures.

Publishing body	Brochure type	Mandatory features, and optional content added by institution.
Tutor Panel	Printed document every two years	professional details of tutors in panel; venues available for study and times; schedule for formal meetings with parents; emergency calls procedures; pupil enrolment details including data required.
Community Resource Centre	Handbook – (annually) with supplements as needed	professional details of warden(s); professional details of specialist tutors; details of societies, clubs for public use; details of all facilities and availability for tutor panels and public & fees; details of foreign exchanges possible.
Field Centre	Handbook - every two years, plus programmes as needed.	professional details of warden; study facilities offered; courses/programmes offered, & fees; accommodation offered, & tariff; features of locality; details of links with field centres abroad.
Central Audio- Visual Education Library	Handbook - four times a year plus frequent supplements.	professional details of all staff - tutorial, production & administration; full cross-referenced listings of resources; explanation of library's work, and philos- ophy underlying programme production.
Middle- Education College	Brochure (annually)	professional details of tutors; details of course types and objectives; details of facilities; availability to the public & fees.
Advanced- Education College	Brochure (annually)	as for Middle-Education colleges.

with considerable detail as to its location and what its locality can offer by way of study or occasional relaxation. Links with field centres abroad will be listed and stressed. The structure of the field centre brochure will be as for the community resource centre and will be revised annually.

All brochures will stress the importance of making contact with, and visiting, other countries. Exchanges, study courses and hobby pursuits can greatly help international relations. Community resource and field centres can enhance opportunities in all these areas by making their networks widely available.

17. Times and venues

Times

There will be no set times for study as there are in the school-based system. Nor will there be school terms, half-terms or school years. Children and tutors will have no prescribed minimum number of hours per week or per year for attendance as at a given school today.

Parents and tutors will agree on the hours most suitable for study having regard to each child's age and disposition and the nature of the work to be done. On this basis they will draw up a schedule for the next week or month. Each party will keep a copy as will the tutor panel chairperson. This schedule-agreement procedure will be part of the contract binding on parent, tutor and state.

There are several advantages in this. Perhaps the most obvious for the population at large is the removal of standardised school hours and the subsequent regular journeys that so often correspond with rush hours. Similarly, the abandonment of school terms and academic years will enable the holidays of children, parents and tutors to be arranged at any time: the scramble, jammed roads, crowds and high prices of Easter, July and August will be a thing of the past.

Much more important, perhaps, is breaking away from the notion understandably held by many adults and children that there are set times for 'education'. Under the teaching-without-schools approach the view will be encouraged that education is an ongoing process which lasts for a lifetime and involves everyone.

Venues

The same will be true of the choice of venue. The idea will be encouraged that it is not only the times of study that are flexible and unlimited, but that places are, too. (See Figure 9 on page 98).

Venues will be agreed between older children, parents and tutors at the same time as, and in conjunction with, the study time schedule. This agreement between parent or guardian on the one hand and the personal tutor or panel chairperson on the other, will be vital to the whole teaching-without-schools enterprise. Parents must know where their children are, with whom they are studying, and when. But, much more than this, they will need to have the same high level of trust in the tutor caring for their children as they have for any other professional person. In this entire parent-tutor relationship unquestioning trust is of the essence. Where such trust is at all in doubt parents will continue to use the old school-based system for their children's education. This system will run for a long time in parallel with the new one. Similarly, a personal tutor who feels she is not wholly accepted by a parent will either avoid situations which might cause unease or decline to enrol that child in her group altogether. However, in the early decades of the new scheme all parents and tutors will be keen volunteers and such lack of faith on either side will be exceptionally rare.

This data will be kept by all parties and filed with the tutor panel chairperson. Thus there will be a careful record kept, one which will always be readily available, to show where a child will be studying, with whom and when, at any given stage in his individual study programme. This regular meeting between parent and tutor to agree time and place schedules will, in itself, be a valuable exercise. It will begin and then extend the working relationship and give both parties something concrete to discuss. Parents who might, in the old school-based system, have been reluctant to make study suggestions to teachers or even to visit the school, will be immersed in the scheduling and programme-content decision-making from the beginning. Both parent and tutor will have an opportunity to get to know each other well. They will have to sit down together and hammer out what is to be done, when and where, for how long, by whom, and why. This essential working-relationship between parent and tutor, and later – as the child grows older – between child, parent and tutor, will need to be started early. It will be the very stuff of the relationship.

Choice of study venue will be wide. Twelve possibilities are:

- Pupils', friends' and tutors' homes.
- Libraries, museums, art galleries, theatres, cinemas and exhibition centres.
- Community resource centres, sports and leisure centres.
- Churches, chapels, cathedrals, abbeys.
- Parks, zoological and botanical and other gardens including arboreta and wild-flower areas.
- County, city, town and village halls, church and chapel halls and others.
- Field centres, youth hostels, youth clubs.
- Houses, gardens and sites of historical interest.

- Craft, agricultural and industrial heritage centres.
- Hotels, motels, caravan and theme parks out of season.
- Trains, canal boats and steamers.
- Universities and colleges during student vacations.

Detailed data files will be kept for tutors' use by CAVEL and will be available from all resource centres. The centre's clerical staff will check on venue availability for tutors or tutor panels and either make reservations or offer alternative dates or venues.

Such variation of venue will increase as children move into their fifth, sixth and seventh age bands and will aid the notion that learning is ubiquitous as well as timeless. Use of facilities in universities and colleges during vacations will introduce children to further learning centres and will help many to explore aspects of higher education – an opportunity which they would not all have had in the old system.

This wider appreciation – or realisation – of opportunities may extend to parents and other family members who accompany groups on study-trips away from home. Or, with their children, they may be awakened to a whole range of field centre holiday possibilities which they might not otherwise have considered. Some of these may well be at field centres abroad and lead to lifelong friendships with people of other countries and cultures.

18. Individual study programmes

Once teachers are freed, by CAVEL, of time-consuming preparation of lessons, they will have more time and energy to give to the personal needs of pupils.

Then, as schools are phased out, teachers will gain further time as the routine administration demands of the school-based system decline. This saved time, too, can be spent directly in contact with children and their families and be helpful in promoting the tutoring profession in a society which is, in many ways, frequently alien to education.

But by far the most important factor in ensuring that teachers, now tutors, can give of their best will be the removal of school-related stress. Occupational stress has increased in many fields, but viewing the figures for teachers anxious to retire early and others suffering psychological illnesses, it seems to be particularly severe among those working in schools.

It is remarkable that this disturbing state of affairs is accepted so lightly. It would appear that something is very wrong in the school-based system, but that authorities are unwilling to confront the situation and examine *thoroughly radical* alternatives which might alleviate many of the problems. The alternative offered in this book would remove school stress from teachers, keep them in the education service, and give them opportunities to make best use of their talents.

Over a period of several weeks, initially, the tutor will assess each child. She will determine his educability level at that time. She will be deciding how much, in his present state, the child is likely to benefit from the educational opportunities open to him. She will be considering ways in which that 'present state' can or should be changed to increase those opportunities and which of those opportunities should be taken. The position will be different for every child in her group and for every child in the tutor panel to which she and the children belong.

Her own testing of a child's language development, particularly reading skills, and of number work, will be seen against previous reports made on the child in either the old school-based system or in the new system or both according to the child's educational history and his age on joining the tutor panel.

This testing of attainment will be seen against the background of the child's cultivated attitudes to learning, his apparent inherent ability, and the degree of support he receives from his family members.

The tutor will be able to examine previous work done by the child in the panel and discuss this and her own assessment of him with his earlier tutors.

The tutor will have long sessions with the child; sometimes parents will be present, sometimes they will not. Sessions can be held in the slightly formal setting of her office or in the more relaxed atmosphere of the resource centre. At the centre many activities will be in progress, and some can be discussed. From the child's point of view this will be done quite casually, but from the tutor's viewpoint deliberately and meaningfully.

In an ideal world it would be possible to discuss with his doctor and health centre staff the child's medical history, and, with any child psychologist who has been involved with him, his mental health and stage of emotional development. This may come one day, but professional reticence and assured confidentiality will most likely mean that in the early years of the new scheme the tutor will have to rely on those records available to her and on what she can glean from the child's parents. But in her assessment of him prior to beginning studies with him, it will be important for her to compile the fullest picture she can. The degree of success she will enjoy later will depend greatly on the accuracy and completeness of this initial picture.

The tutor can then discuss with the child (depending on his age) and with his parents, the work she is to do. She will incorporate suggestions and requests where these accord with her assessment of needs and explain why others might be inappropriate at that time. Knowing both the importance of this and how, tactfully, to execute it, will be a much-needed skill and one emphasised and taught during professional training. Awareness of the child's earlier tutors' experiences with the parents will be valuable but should not dominate her assessment or lead to her prejudgement of her pupil.

With this information to hand the tutor will be able to draft, in some detail, a year's study programme. This will be divided into stages of months or weeks according to what she thinks best for the child.

This draft will be taken back to the family and discussed and amended as suits the situation. The tutor may, before or after discussion with the child's family, confer with colleagues, especially with the tutor panel chairperson. She will check the availability of facilities she is likely to need, particularly the several lesson unit series she will need from CAVEL.

She will, before drafting the basic study programme, have estimated how much co-operation she and the child will receive from the family; how much time and other resources they will contribute, and how reliable, long-term, this is likely to be. She will allow for help brothers and sisters will be able to give according to how well she or other tutors in the tutor panel know them.

The accuracy of the tutor's assessment will depend partly on her years of experience, but assessment of educability procedures will have been covered intensively in her professional training.

Also vital will be the tutor's knowledge of what is available to help her in her work with her client. She must have familiarity with the multimedia source material, whether from CAVEL, the Internet or elsewhere, knowledge of the facilities of her community resource centre and local field centres, and of the locations of other available venues together with details of the help they can offer. She will need to know of the specialisms of consultants working within the education service or of those who can be brought in from outside, and of ways of finding out what aid is available or what can be done if a child's progress is worryingly slow.

In her new role as personal tutor, as opposed to classroom teacher, she will be seen more as the equivalent of a general medical practitioner who prescribes what she believes to be best from her knowledge of what is available from her resources and what is reasonably acceptable and attainable by the patient. To take the medical parallel further, there will be no benefit to the patient from a powerful new remedy available for eczema if the doctor has not kept up with her reading and knows nothing about it, or if she does not realise that her patient is allergic to the new drug or is in some other way beyond its help. Similarly the personal tutor will need to know what can best be done, as new study units are developed, for each child in her care. The responsibility will be great.

Copies of the child's study programme will be given to the child if he is old enough, to the parents always, and to the tutor panel chairperson for information and filing. The programme will be presented as a whole but will be constructed

Figure 12. Children's individual study programmes.

People involved	Basic processes
Personal tutor leads discussions with parents (and children old enough to understand) to discern needs and determine overall content of two-year programme.	● tutor outlines two-year work plan; ● age, ability, educability, interests and parental wishes influence draft; ● previous tutoring and level of attainment examined and allowed for; ● facilities available for study and parental attitude to education considered.
Personal tutor, with child's previous tutors, specialist tutors and resource centre staff – all as and when required.	● tutor presents draft of two-year plan; ● shows plan broken down into manageable units based on days, weeks, months; ● indicates topics to be included; literacy, numeracy, and the arts foremost; ● seeks opinions of colleagues as required.
Personal tutor, parents, older children, and tutor panel chairperson as required and resource centre warden as required.	● tutor examines draft, in detail, with parents (and older pupils); ● tutor listens, discusses, amends; ● further meetings – with colleagues present if needed and if parents agreeable; further amendment. ● at formal meeting tutor and parents agree programme and sign contract.
Tutor, parents and, where old enough, child.	● tutor proposes first month's study giving times, venues, CAVEL programmes as agreed by parties; ● parties agree areas of responsibility for all parts of programme for the two year period; ● tutor arranges further meetings as needed.

in such a way that it can be split readily into manageable segments both of study time and curriculum content. According to the tutor's estimate of the child's whole learning environment, she will suggest how much time is to be spent on any segment and how many segments should be attempted in any one day, week or month. This easily manageable structure will be an essential characteristic of each new study programme.

Another characteristic of the study programme will be that it allows the child to do some work on his own, some with the tutor, some with a parent, some with tutor and parent, some with another child, some within a small group of children and some within the tutor's whole group of twenty children. This variation in study practices is vital for ensuring there is time each week for the child to work alone quietly, and other times when he will meet, play and work with other children and have opportunities to make friends outside his own family circle. The valuable friend-making function of many a traditional school and the chance it sometimes gives to each child to experience personal relationships with children of different interests, background and personality must never be lost in the new educational system. But the unhappiness – sometimes intense – of those children who encounter bullying, taunting, isolation or sometimes inexplicable unpopularity in school must not be tolerated.

Further, it will be important to ensure that study takes place in several quite different venues and for different periods of time. This might range from forty minutes on his own with the tutor to several days with nineteen other children plus parents and tutors at a distant field centre in an environment unlike the one in which he lives and usually studies.

The activities envisaged in the study programme will include items ranging from those which require as intense a concentration as the child can manage, to those which offer enjoyable relaxation and the opportunity to pursue hobbies, interests and social intercourse of the child's own choosing.

Further deliberately engineered provision in the study programme will ensure that there is a balance between sedentary study and physical activity. The latter will not be restricted to the physical education associated with the school-based system which is sometimes disliked by a sizeable proportion of pupils. It will include such activities as gardening, hiking, delivering greetings or meals to the elderly or disabled in the local community.

Time will be allowed for the older pupil to undertake projects of his own design or those suggested by parents. He will be able to continue these from stage to stage and tutor to tutor as current programmes are reviewed or new ones compiled. Some pupils will be eager to take interests begun this way into middle and higher education and to continue with them for years beyond that.

A prime long-term objective of working through individual study plans will be first to encourage and then to enable pupils to study on their own without supervision. Help will always be available including suggestions for further progress, references, ideas, sources and the names of people outside the tutor panel who can advise. But ultimately a significant measure of success of the teaching-children-without-schools approach will be the extent to which the pupil who completes early education is able to review and assess his own individual study programme and develop it further for himself. Those will be skills which he can take with him to the next stage of his education. Such skills will be linked inextricably to the emphasis given to wholehearted preparation for the increasing amount of 'free' or 'non-working' or 'leisure' time that many people in future generations will enjoy.

Because of this it will be necessary, before drawing up study programmes and before discussing with parents programme content and teaching method, to:

● Help the child and his family acknowledge the extent to which work patterns will change and to alter the belief, still held by some, that education can or should guarantee a job for life.

● Approach this 'fact of economic life' positively and accept that early retirement could offer flexibility and the chances of a better lifestyle that was not available to previous generations when forty to fifty years at the same monotonous and sometimes unhealthy job was not unusual.

● Introduce pupils to a variety of pursuits, encouraging them to concentrate on those they particularly enjoy, which might give rise to long-term interest and pleasure.

● Understand the value of travel abroad and the facilities available to people to travel extensively by means of the international network of study and recreational centres available.

19. Tutors' professional status

The change of title from 'teacher' to 'tutor' will be deliberate. It will be purposeful, not cosmetic. It will focus attention sharply on a basic change in role. With it will come an improved service for the client and enhanced status for the provider.

The Oxford Dictionary defines a 'teacher' as one who trains or instructs in a skill, or as one who gives lessons. This is far too narrow a concept for the new role. But the same dictionary's definition of 'tutor', as one who has general charge of a person's education and who directs the studies of those assigned to him, will be accurate.

The example, in some of the older universities, of tutors who see their students singly or in small groups and who arrange work for the student, discuss it and generally supervise his studies, is a useful one.

The same system applied to children will enable the personal tutor to base her work in her own home or that of a colleague and to see her pupils with or without parents in small groups for an hour or more several times a week in order to get to know them as persons, to introduce them to new ideas, open up new perspectives on old ideas and, with parents, to supervise the studies she has prescribed.

This freedom to plan her own and her clients' work, to select material and suggest activities based on it, together with the authority to arrange her own schedules and stipulate her workplace entirely free of hierarchical dictates will raise the status of the tutor in her own eyes and in those of the community.

Such unprecedented freedom in her work alongside increased responsibility, accountability and direct contact with parents, will make the role a professional one. The personal tutor, with her own pupil group, will be the crux of the whole new service. This will be quite contrary to the position in the school-based system where the 'ordinary' unpromoted class or assistant teacher attracts the poorest salary, suffers the lowest status, experiences confrontation, endures stress, and exercises least influence in educational decision-making. It remains to be seen whether current proposals (January, 1999) to raise the classteacher's status actually come into effect, but certainly, as the 20th century closes, the classteacher's position in Britain is not an enviable one.

While in the new system of teaching-without-schools the tutor will still be the general practitioner, she will be that in her own right. *She will have no liege but her clients.*

If the tutor follows the usual career pattern she will work for thirty-five years, from age twenty-five to sixty. She will then retire on two-thirds of final salary. If she wishes she may, after this, and with tutor panel approval, give additional help to a panel on a temporary, part-time basis.

During that full-length career the tutor will be professionally involved with some fifteen personal groups, tutoring each group for two years. For four or five years – perhaps more for some tutors – she will have no tutor group responsibility. For those times she might be acting as tutor panel chairperson, be working at CAVEL, or be on study-leave researching or attending courses at home or abroad. This varied activity will be beneficial for the tutor and her pupils, and be an excellent development for the emerging profession. Tutors wishing to study or to teach courses abroad, or give a series of lectures, will be encouraged to do so and be given financial help. Every opportunity will be taken to make such tours and exchanges fruitful.

With no non-teaching superiors controlling her from within an imposed hierarchy, and with jurisdiction over her own work, the tutor will have a far higher status than her assistant-teacher predecessor. But, at the same time, she will have to accept responsibility for the decisions she makes regarding her pupils' educational progress. There will be no-one to whom she can pass the buck.

The only possible exception to this professional liability will be those occasions when a parent is unable to accept a proposed line of study for his child yet does not want to change his child's tutor or tutor panel. Here the tutor may reach a compromise and amend the study programme if she feels the revised schedule will be less harmful to the pupil than a complete change of tutor or panel. But she will indicate that she cannot be held solely responsible if the revised programme is not wholly successful. She will notify the panel chairperson of this disagreement and the resultant compromise. She will record the changes made and the reasons for them.

In cases where differences remain, the tutor will encourage formal consultation between herself, the parents, the panel chairperson and others concerned with the child's development. These 'others' might be previous tutors or agencies in the medical, psychological, probationary or special education fields.

A child's personal needs in these latter areas will be more readily identifiable in a long-term small-group system where tutors have training in procedures for early identification of difficulties, and have access to and knowledge of the family and its social circumstances. It will be impossible for a pupil's problems to escape notice unless a tutor is singularly unobservant, incompetent or negligent.

But normally the position will be a great advance on the stressful school-based system. Parents' growing confidence in the tutor's professional integrity will encourage disclosure of problems whether these are personal or academic, or both. At present, teachers' best efforts in these areas are too often hampered by demands made on them for class control and for ever-improving test and examination results. Then both these demands are often compounded by hierarchical school regimes or imposed teaching modes, and the requirements of an inspection system that lays insufficient emphasis on the all-important matter of long-term teacher-pupil relationships. When this is added to the strain of managing thirty or more pupils for thirty hours a week it is understandable that the talents and problems of shy, nervous children and others are sometimes overlooked.

There is the further very sensitive point that the assistant teacher, her day already full, feels that those staff members on higher salary levels and with lighter teaching loads are better placed to cope with the time-consuming personal difficulties of her own class members. But this is not necessarily the ideal way forward because child and senior staff member may not know each other well enough. Inhibitions associated with 'rank' too, may detract from the value of such encounters.

The fault rarely lies with any one pupil or teacher, it is more likely to be inherent in the school-based system. Schools are often too big, attempt too many things, and are available to pupils and parents for too few hours during the year. The whole school edifice restricts what the teacher can do, needs to do and wants to do.

In the new approach these constraints will disappear. All three parties – pupils, parents and tutors – will enjoy freedom of action. There will be considerable choice in all aspects of the tutoring process.

Parents will choose a tutor for their children and the tutor will have some say in the choice of her pupils and colleagues. As children grow older they will make important choices in the work they do and sometimes when necessary, in their choice of tutor.

Change of tutor will be initiated if the parent feels dissatisfied with progress being made, or is in disagreement with the tutor's aims and methods, or if there are personality conflicts which may impede the child's social and educational development. But if the tutor has done her preparatory work properly these instances should be rare.

The tutor will decline to continue working with a pupil for whom she feels she has nothing further to offer, or one who fails persistently to make progress through lack of effort, poor attitude or lack of parental co-operation. Eventually, and for the wellbeing of the child, the tutor will be able to say to recalcitrant pupils and their unhelpful parents:

"I am sorry, but this is getting us nowhere. It isn't helping anyone. You will be best advised to choose another tutor panel where methods, facilities and personalities will be more to your liking. Please seek a transfer to another panel. If you are not sure of how to go about this, these are the names of people at the local community resource centre who will be able to help you..."

The resource centre warden and staff will provide tutor lists and tutor panel addresses, and will help parents who need it to make application for their child to be considered for admission to another tutor panel. Where appropriate, they will arrange an interview with the new tutor panel chairperson.

The tutor will have some choice of colleagues as well as of pupils. The tutor panel she applies to join will be one of her own selection and, in turn, tutors in the panel will decide whether she is an applicant likely to be compatible with themselves and their ways of working. The length of time a tutor spends with a panel will be as long as is mutually beneficial. Short periods of service with a panel will be discouraged because of the lack of continuity in work they cause. Also they will make the panel less attractive to perceptive parents.

In addition to career freedom, the tutor will find that her salary will be as high as or higher than that of any other worker in the education service. There will be no person, whether researcher, administrator or CAVEL programme-producer, who will earn more money or command more prestige. The experienced personal tutor who is engaged in the prime task of tutoring children will be the pivotal person in the system and always she will be regarded as such.

As there will be no exception to this status and salary ruling there will be no expectations among entrants to the profession that the task of tutoring is something to be undertaken until 'promotion' to better-paid and more prestigious work within the service is secured. There will be no such promotion. In stark contrast to the career-structure of the school-based system, a movement away from tutoring will be seen as a sideways or downwards step to other forms of work in the educational field. Additional salary will be earned only by the tutor gaining higher professional qualifications combined with wider and appropriate tutoring experience. Any such 'bonus' or additional salary will be on terms agreed with the tutor's professional body, the Professional Tutors Guild (PTG).

Early education tutors will occasionally work in areas of further education and, if this is in addition to their normal work, they will be paid extra. Such work may be long-term participation in a major course or assistance with tutorials in an area in which the tutor has expert knowledge or special experience.

Tutor panel chairpersons, during their two years in office, will be entitled to three months' leave of absence on full salary to research or develop a topic of interest to them and which will benefit their pupils later. A chairperson may travel abroad, study privately, work on curriculum development, draft a book or submit programme ideas for CAVEL's consideration. By mutual consent she can extend this period of leave if the work begun merits further time. This provision will end the present situation in Britain whereby a teacher can work for thirty or forty years, teaching large classes for the whole of that time, and have no entitlement to an extended study leave.

Further, during a full career, each tutor will be able to take a sabbatical year some time after her tenth year of service and a second after twenty years. This will be public money well spent as the renewal of energy and skills made possible will be of immense value to children and parents later. It will be a recognition of the demanding nature of tutoring work when such work is performed conscientiously for a long time.

But these will be minor rewards for the tutor when compared with the satisfaction of being able to influence a pupil's choice of studies and then guide and supervise his work. All will affect the quality of life the pupil is enabled to lead. The tutor will be able to feed ideas, suggest alternative ways of living, and indicate values which should be prized.

It may be that she will offer an upbringing even richer and more varied than that experienced already by children from caring and well-educated families. She will be able to do this with her small pupil groups and pupils' parents in ways that suit her way of working best.

Figure 13. Personal tutors' careers and responsibilities.

	Ten Factors	Details
1	Basic qualifications:	● University honours degree; ● L.P.T.G.: Licentiate of the Professional Tutors Guild, awarded only by the PTG.
2	Years of training:	● 3 or 4 years for bachelor's degree; ● 3 years (minimum) for L.P.T.G.
3	Approximate ages at start:	● Minimum: 25. ● Maximum: 44 or 45 (for mature entrants).
4	Likely length of career:	● 35 years if career uninterrupted. ● 20 years to gain pension on retirement.

5	In-service training:	● Frequent, ranging from short courses to full
		   sabbatical year-long studies;
		● All training will be organised, approved and
		   largely provided by the PTG with exchange
		   arrangements with similar professional bodies
		   abroad.

6	Skills required:	● Largely inherent ability, enhanced by training,
		   to relate easily to others;
		● Ability to explain clearly, to all abilities and
		   ages, the basics and purposes of any study unit;
		● Ability to discuss real – as opposed to imagined
		   – needs and to provide for them;
		● Ability to utilise modern educational technology
		   and to extract benefits from it.

7	Hours of work:	● Averaging 48 hours per week as required; ● 6 weeks annual leave plus sabbaticals.
8	Client contact:	● Each pupil seen (on average) 3 times a week; ● Personal group seen (on average) 3 times a week; ● Parents seen (on average) once a week.
9	Responsibility assumed to clients:	● To child: very high, higher than for any other professional person; ● To parent: high, equal to other professionals; ● To state: high incidental responsibility.
10	Social value of tutors' work:	● To child: beyond any reasonable assessment; ● To parent: very high; to some indispensable; ● To state: high – providing for future generations.

Perhaps the most urgent message she will deliver to them will be that a happy, satisfying life can be led simply and led without those annual demands for increasing money wages which lead eventually to the consumption of more and more of the world's limited resources. Little could be more important than that. Eventually, whatever education system is adopted in any nation, helping people to realise that there has to be a limit to material aspirations will become a cornerstone of responsible policy.

With her close relationship with her pupils the tutor will be well-placed to further that philosophy in a quiet, unassuming, matter-of-fact, kindly, non-threatening yet effective way. It will be a way of working which will match the nature of the objective sought: a peaceful, kind and protected world. And it is a way of working that changes beneficially the current role of schoolteacher.

This gradual change in role is illustrated in Figure 14 on page 125. In the first 30 years (i.e. one generation) of the 21st century normal school-orientated teacher-training continues but steadily declines as more young graduates opt for tutorial work within the new non-school system. In the second generation such 'normal' teacher-training has ended, schools have declined sharply in numbers and a network of community resource centres and field centres is almost complete; the bulk of the profession is practising tutorially, and CAVEL is fully on stream. With the third generation, 2060 to 2099, there are personal tutors for 99% of 0 to 14 year olds, and the tutoring profession is fully established, self-regulating, highly regarded and attracting sufficient candidates of a consistently high calibre to ensure its high-status future.

20. Tutors' professional education

Selection

The minimum age for practising as a fully-qualified personal tutor will be twenty-five. After three years at university reading for an honours degree there will be four years of professional education of which two years will be probationary work, under supervision, with personal groups. While reading for her degree the student will not be committed to tutoring as a career and will be funded by the usual grants, loans or awards available to all students. Later, during her four years of professional training, she will be paid a salary based on a four-year pro-bationary-tutors' scale. Retrospectively this service will be recognised as pensionable once the student qualifies and begins her tutoring career.

A first or second class honours degree in any subject area will be required before a graduate can apply for training as a personal tutor. She will then be invited to informal talks with tutor panel chairpersons and resource centre

Figure 14. Changes in tutor role and recruitment over three generations.

Decade Beginning	Teacher-tutor professional education and training.	Transfer, redeployment and training of other professionals.	Professional training of tutors (if new scheme is adopted).
2000	Teacher volunteers sought for pilot scheme alongside normal recruitment and training of majority.		
2010			
2020	Training emphasis is now on preparation for the new profession of tutoring. Teacher training is phased out.	Voluntary retraining of graduate or (equivalent) probation- officers, nurses, doctors, lawers, accountants. etc.	Many of those who would, in 1999, have entered other professions now consider and take up an alternative career in tutoring – on leaving university.
2030			
2040			
2050			
2060	By third generation the new profession of tutoring is fully established and highly qualified; highly paid tutors assist parents with the education of children from birth to the age of 14.		
2070			
2080			
2090	Combination of tutoring with other social services is now fully developed.		

wardens. These talks will be largely for the candidate's benefit. They will offer information and advice on the rigours of training and the rewarding but demanding nature of the professional practice which follows.

If she remains interested the candidate will make formal application to a regional office of the Professional Tutors' Guild (PTG) to be registered as a tutorial student. This formal registration will impress upon her, as well as on parents and others, that the PTG will be the body concerned with her training and with the eventual granting of membership of the Guild. This membership will confer on her the right to practise in the profession. Membership will be difficult to attain and attainment of it will be mandatory for all professional personal tutors.

Each regional PTG will have an initial-training committee, one of whose duties will be to assess applications and contact referees. Obligatory among a candidate's referees will be (i) the university tutor best known to her, (ii) the personal tutor of her principal subject at university and (iii) her personal tutor in her last year of study before university. Unless all three give favourable reports on her character and her academic work her application will go no further. Two other referees of the candidate's choice must give assurances of her personal suitability for the work ahead.

A candidate whose references are satisfactory will attend a series of interviews lasting a week, and will be accommodated in a resource centre or field centre. Two days will be spent with a tutor group observing the work and in discussing pupils' needs and attainments. Three days will be spent working in the accommodating resource or field centre and in visiting other personal groups. There will be one day writing-up what has been seen, with comment. This written work will be discussed later at the interviews. Then, on the last day, there will be a series of formal group and individual interviews with a PTG appointments committee. This committee will comprise a personal tutor, a chairperson, a resource centre warden, two regional PTG officers and two parent representatives from local government.

Apart from delving into the candidate's background, seeking reasons for her wanting to become a tutor, considering reports written on her during the week and discussing her own written commentary, each committee member will be asked to put to himself or herself one basic question:

"From what I now know of her, do I want this applicant to become a personal tutor so that she can work with and influence many young people and, perhaps, their families, for the next thirty or forty years?" Members will be able to respond "Yes", "No", or "Not sure".

The candidate will need to get "Yes" from at least five of the seven members and a "Not sure" from one of the others. If it so chooses, the committee can offer another interview a year later to a candidate who gains four votes of "Yes" and two of "Not sure".

126

While this might seem to be a lengthy, costly and elaborate procedure, the importance of the initial selection cannot be over-estimated. Candidates' suitability for the task of tutoring the next generation must be beyond all reasonable doubt. Selection of students for teacher-training in the old school-based system was often less thorough. Stringent efforts in selection will be needed in future if public confidence in the new profession is to be established and then maintained.

A four-stage course of training

For the first stage of the course, after she has obtained her honours degree and been accepted for training by the PTG board, the student will spend six months at a university school of tutorial training on an intensive introductory course. Areas covered will include:

● Child development from conception to age fourteen years.
● The concept of educability and the interaction of its components.
● Literacy and numeracy needs as related to the 21st century and the curricular implications of this.
● The scope of computer-based and multimedia learning, and safeguards against its abuse.
● Curriculum development and the use of individual study programmes.
● Establishing and maintaining satisfactory and positive relationships between tutor, pupil and parent.
● Social values and value-transmission in contemporary society.
● Problems relating to family life which arise from both within and without the family.
● Childhood problems, insecurity, fear and abuse, dealing with these, and the involvement of associated outside agencies.
● The importance in early-education of using opportunities for furthering international understanding.

There will be oral and written pass-fail examinations in each area and all will need to be passed at the end of the six-month period. Re-sits will be allowed in one or two areas if exceptionally high marks have been gained elsewhere and if the visiting tutors and university staff concerned are in agreement. At no time will any university be required to pass a percentage or quota of students: students will be passed on merit only.

Successful students will proceed to stage two, where they will spend a year working with four personal tutor groups, staying for three months with each.

Figure 15. Personal tutors' education and training.

Stage	Description	Years	Principal content(s).
1	School/college 6th Form 'A' levels (GCE).	2	Preference for most students to take literature and other arts subjects.
2	University: 1st or 2nd class honours degree.	3 or 4	Preference for majority to read arts or social sciences.
3	University: studying for Licentiate of the Professional Tutors Guild (Part I).	1	Parent/family studies; theory of education relating to babyhood, early and later childhood; supervised observation of tutorial groups.
4	University: studying for LPTG (Part II).	1	Supervised studies during fieldwork with: 4 different personal groups covering 4 different age groups; collection of material for thesis.
5	University: studying for LPTG (Part III).	1	Intensive tutorials with tutor and the writing and submission of thesis based on material obtained in previous year. By arrangement some of this time can be spent abroad.
6	Probationary period of tutoring on successful completion of which the LPTG is awarded.	2	Tutorial supervision of one two-year stage of a tutor-group's education with the co-operation of the tutor-panel chairperson who will report back to the student-tutor's university.
7	In-service training and professional development. Entitlement to one or two sabbaticals.		Ongoing training throughout career aimed at up-dating tutor on research developments, and providing periods away from the intensive work within a tutor-panel.

Alongside this will be study within the university in which the practical work will be reviewed and the educational theory carefully related to it. Seminar papers will be produced by student tutors and assessed by themselves, their peers and their supervising tutor.

The four tutor groups attended will be in different tutor-panels so that the experience gained will be wide. The early-education stages selected for each student-tutor will include band one – the birth to second birthday stage, and band seven – the twelve to fourteenth birthday stage, plus two other consecutive stages of the student's choice.(See p.78 for details of the 7 two-year stages).

The student-tutor must obtain satisfactory reports from each of the four personal tutors with whom she works, and from her visiting, supervising university tutor. The supervisor will liaise with tutor panel chairpersons. The supervisor will also maintain the student-tutor's contact with the university and arrange her ongoing work there.

Failure to obtain five satisfactory reports and to complete satisfactorily the work set at the university will normally mean withdrawal from the course. But with four good reports and one inadequate one the student-tutor will have her position considered by a PTG adjudication committee with a view to possible course extension.

The student who remains in training for the third stage will spend six months at university preparing, under supervision, a thesis. That will be on a topic of her choice which arose from her practical experience in the previous year. To be approved, the topic must be one that calls on the student-tutor to visit additional groups, or involves other practical work in order to obtain further data for inclusion in the thesis. It may relate to the subsequent middle or further education stage, or be connected with the development of continuing education and leisure interests in the general population. Whenever possible, and without compromising the need for tutor group visits, some of this work may be conducted abroad.

On successful completion of the first three stages the student-tutor will be awarded provisional or associate membership of the PTG and will be allowed to practise, under supervision, for two years. This will be the equivalent of a trainee doctor's medical practice in a hospital. She will join a tutor-panel as a probationary personal tutor. Usually she will help to tutor one personal group of pupils through one two-year stage and release their tutor, for some of that time, to do different work in the panel or relieve other tutors for in-service study, or take local in-service training herself.

The probationary student-tutor will be under the general guidance of the panel chairperson who will report monthly on her progress to the regional PTG board. In that way, with such frequent reporting, problems can be detected and addressed at an early stage.

At the end of that two year period, when the PTG committee is entirely satisfied with the reports filed, the probationer will be accorded full professional membership of the Guild. In exceptional circumstances the committee may recommend an extension of probation for a further year. If the extension is granted the probationer will spend the extra year working in a different tutor panel in a different resource centre area; thus she will experience a different locality and different personnel and be given a fresh assessment. There will be no further extension should her failure be repeated and she will not be registered as a qualified personal tutor.

As soon as circumstances permit, i.e. sufficient other countries adopt the teaching-without-schools approach to education, at least six months of the four years of tutor-training will need to be spent in another country. This will be in addition to any time the student spent abroad while studying for her first degree or on vacation work. While these earlier periods will have been invaluable in themselves, the professional training period spent abroad will be linked directly to childhood education in personal family groups. The dual purpose will be to broaden the student's own outlook so that she becomes a more interesting, knowledgeable tutor, and to further international understanding and co-operation – which will be for the good of everyone.

5. The Next Stage

Middle-education colleges

14 to 16

In their last year of early-education and well before their fourteenth birthday, pupils will consult with parents and tutors on the studies they wish to follow during their four years of continuing education: the next stage.

The first part of this will be two years of middle-education, taken at a middle-education college, and the second will be two years of advanced-education at an advanced-education college, at ages 14-16, and 16-18 respectively.

Some temporary work in the colleges will be undertaken by personal tutors from early-education. This will:

● Assist with the continuity of pupil care.

● Provide early-education tutors with information on what their pupils will be doing at their next stage of education.

● Give those early-education tutors some variety of professional experience by enabling them to teach older pupils.

● Enable the tutors to teach their subject or special interest to a higher level.

● Be entirely voluntary, i.e. early-education tutors will elect to do this work.

No examinations will be held at the end of early-education. Instead, with the agreement of pupil and parent, there will be available to interested parties detailed records of a child's studies for his final two years. These records will have been prepared by his personal tutor, and, in addition to this, his fourteen early-education years will have been summarised formally by the tutor-panel chairperson in co-operation with the child's parents.

Nothing will be published without the approval of the pupil and his parents, but the reports will be available, confidentially and for professional reasons, to his new personal tutor at middle-education college. The pupil and his parents will receive copies of the fourteen-year summary for their retention and use.

The compilation of this summary will test the professionalism of tutors. While nothing must be omitted which they think is relevant to the child's well-being, and nothing included which is not merited, the final version, which may take a long time to complete, will be made with the help of pupil and parent. Parents will have been made aware of this continuous assessment procedure throughout the fourteen early-education years. How far parents accept the integrity of tutors in making this final report will be a reflection on the whole early-education process. Parents will know that a bland, uncommitted summary will be of little value to anyone – least of all to their child.

For all pupils the summary will indicate the level of attainment in language and number work, specific interests which have been followed, attitude to work, contributions made to personal group life and to the needs of the wider community in which the child's family lives.

At the close of early education there may be a tiny minority of pupils for whom further education at a college is inappropriate and for whom continuing tutorial study at a personal level would be more suitable. Arrangements will be made for these young people to be tutored individually or in small groups by tutors from the colleges which the students would attend and of which they will still be full, facility-enjoying members. Such students may be exceptionally gifted in a particular field, or of very low all-round ability, or may have particular physical or psychological problems which would make college life and work unsuitable for them and unhappy for them and their fellow students. Their college personal tutor will arrange for these students to have specialised and mostly individualised tuition, and this will continue until age eighteen.

At first, the colleges of middle and advanced-education will be established in existing further education colleges, sixth-form colleges, upper schools or large comprehensive schools retained from the old system. They will be adapted to meet the new needs.

There will be liaison between the colleges and the community resource centres and field centres whose facilities the college staff will use in their work.

Financially the colleges will be the joint responsibility of the regional education authorities and central government. Staffing will be the responsibility of a staffing committee in each college. On these committees college tutors will always be in a majority.

Tutors will be appointed on the basis of anticipated demand for the course or subjects offered by the candidate and the personal acceptability of the applicant as a prospective colleague. Where the quality of candidates is unacceptable no appointment will be made, no courses in that subject area will be offered, and an enquiry will be established to determine the cause of the shortfall. It will never be permissible to lower tutor standards so that inadequately-qualified staff can fill tutor posts. If salaries and conditions of work need to be improved, then improved they will have to be.

No college tutor will have life tenure. Seven-year contracts will be awarded so that, eventually, one seventh of each college's staff will be reapplying for appointment each year. Contracts will be renewed in the light of each tutor's work, her further-study record, and the demand for the courses she has to offer.

A quarter of staff will work part-time, some for as little as an hour a week. This will enable tutors to be appointed who have a specialism required only occasionally by a few students. But, equally important, it will allow tutors from early-education panels to work occasionally on courses with older, more

Figure 16. Education after age fourteen.

Stage and age	Students	Courses and assessments
Middle-education College Ages 14-16	All early-education leavers except for some 5% who may receive separate personal tuition as a continuation of early-education.	Each student takes 10 units of study. At least two must be taken from each of four basic categories: ● the arts ● sciences ● social sciences ● leisure Assessment will be by course work and final interview. *A completion of studies certificate,* with tutorial comment will be issued to all students at age 16+.
Advanced Education College Ages 16-18+	All middle-education leavers except for some 5% to 10% who may be permitted to spend up to 80% of their time on community work. All students will receive an Advanced Education College (AEC) grant and none will work for another wage in other employment.	One unit of study from each of the same four categories above plus one from each of two other categories: ● occupational skills ● international studies plus a 7th unit as agreed with the tutor. Assessment will be by course-work, examination and interview. *A completion of studies certificate,* with grades, will be awarded to all students at age 18+.
Adult Education Ages 18+ (No upper age limit)	After 18 all students will follow one of three routes for at least three years on a full-time basis.	1. University degree course; 2. Vocational training; 3. Community service; All routes will attract a three-year adult student maintenance grant.

advanced students. These early-education tutors will take their skills to the colleges and, at the same time, establish links with the colleges which will be of benefit to their own early-education pupils.

As with early-education panels, and resource and field centres, colleges will publish brochures detailing their courses, tutors' qualifications and experience, and their general facilities. Personal tutors and panel chairpersons will study these carefully with their early-education pupils and make arrangements for lengthy visits to the colleges during their pupils' final year. They will then be able to assist with the preparation of their personal pupils' initial work schedules for use in their first period at the middle-education college.

Places on undersubscribed courses will be offered to other members of the community at an economic fee. Again, the presence of students from different age groups will benefit everyone.

In both middle and advanced-education colleges the courses offered and assessed will fall into one of four categories:

1. Courses in which emphasis will be on the development of academic study and intellectual skills including mathematics and science.

2. Courses in which some studies will be built around current international, national and local issues and include further development of social values.

3. Courses in which studies will be aimed at helping, in practical ways, the college as a whole and the wider community in which it works.

4. Courses aimed at developing the leisure interests of students; these may include learning one or more foreign languages and relate to the international studies (category six) course to be taken at the advanced education college.

These four categories will be known as:

1. Arts and general sciences.   3. Community studies and services.
2. Social sciences.   4. Leisure interests.

On entering a middle-education college at age fourteen, each pupil will select ten units of study which he will follow for two years. He will take two topics from each of the four categories above, and two from any other category or categories he chooses. These last two may be from ready-made college courses (supported again by CAVEL) or be courses constructed by the student and his tutor. In the first category English language must be taken as one of the units by all students and the work in this unit will be largely literature based.

Thus an academically-able student will be able to take English plus three academic subject units in category one, and add one or two social science units from category two, making six academic studies in all. Several of these may be continued through advanced education college and then on to university.

A less-academic pupil will be able to offer six units from categories three and four plus English and three other units from the first two categories.

Work will be graded in all units and the levels achieved by each student will be indicated on the leaving certificate awarded at age sixteen, together with testimonial comment on his personal approach to study. There will be no pass/fail grades or final examination: coursework will be assessed in units as completed.

Advanced-education colleges
16 to 18

For advanced-education the course organisation will be similar to that in middle-education but, where appropriate and after discussion with parents and previous tutors, fewer units will be studied and these will be taken to higher levels.

The same four categories as in middle-education colleges will be available in advanced education plus two others. These will be occupational skills (category five) which will offer introductions to many possible future employment fields, and international studies (category six) which will involve the student in the close study of a nation different from his own and in which nation he will spend at least three months of his two-year advanced education course.

The number of units taken for the two years will be reduced to seven. One unit will be taken from each of the six categories already listed plus any one other chosen by the student and approved by his tutor. The future university student will still have the option of five academic subjects, as before, and can, if he wishes, follow the five he began in middle-education. Students can, on the other hand, select two units from category five and one from each of the remaining four and so create a curriculum which would be largely non-academic.

There will be coursework grades and a final written examination in all category one units. The latter will be at the level of and graded in the same way as the current GCE 'A' level papers and will meet university entrance requirements for honours degree courses.

Again, unfilled places on courses will be offered to people in older age groups and, once accepted for a unit place, that place will be ensured for the full two-year period regardless of fluctuations in student numbers.

The final certificate, issued at age eighteen or above, will be more comprehensive than the summary given at sixteen and will assess performance attainment and effort made for each unit taken. There will be a character reference written by the student's personal tutor after consultation with the student and his parents. Full and detailed records will be kept at the college for ten years and these will be seen by the student, future employers and other persons to whom the student grants reading permission. On her nomination by the student, confidential references – which will not be seen by the student – can be given by the student's final year personal tutor.

6. Administration

Looking ahead

An enabling role

If the new system is widely extended there will need to be an administrative structure designed to facilitate, but not control, the tutors' work.

There will be a regional board consisting of elected members drawn from a number of counties; this will help to diminish disproportionate influence by any one highly-politicised county or city council.

Members of a regional board consisting of elected members drawn from town or county councillors, local branches of the Professional Tutors' Guild, the universities, local parents' associations, representatives from foreign professional tutors' guilds, and two 'observing-only' members from central government.

The regional board will be advised by four sub-committees whose recommendations it will usually ratify. The four sub-committees will be advising on early, middle, advanced and adult education respectively. On all committees there will be a majority of practising tutors. They will have the power to co-opt non-voting members from such areas as the police, the probation service, welfare agencies, the churches, and the medical, engineering and accountancy professions.

While each sub-committee's work will vary, all will consider the wider social and ethical implications of the advised curriculum and will receive reports from resource centre wardens about work done locally. They will be anxious to support good work done at home and abroad by tutors, especially that which furthers the acceptance by young people of the moral values implicit in that work, and which, in any way possible, promotes international understanding and the notion of a one-world society.

This encouragement of the transmission of agreed values will be imperative for successful socialisation. It will be in marked contrast to some of the partisan activities of some politically-motivated committees which have overseen the school-based system. An example of this has been the use of the grammar schools as footballs, kicked around by opposing ideologies. Political correctness and ill-disguised social engineering have seemed, at times, to be more important than the personal development of the individual child, or the legitimate concerns of his parents, or the earnest work of his teachers, or even the upholding of moral and social standards.

Under the new teaching-without-schools approach committees will review work undertaken in other regions and abroad and will consider whether this has implications for the educational work being done in their own locality. But when considering new ideas they will bear in mind the need to support tutors in their work of upholding agreed social values. As they develop, older pupils themselves must be helped to realise that the quality of life for everyone deteriorates when the fabric of society is weakened by those who abide only by the rules they choose to accept and then only when it suits them, or who, in time of need, seek the benefits of membership when they have for many years eschewed the accordant responsibilities or the need to make ongoing contributions of time, effort and money to that society's wellbeing.

In the new system tutors' work will not be subject to change every time there is a political shift in power or when some new doctrine is ushered in and an old one thrown out. In the teaching-without-schools organisation there will be little which can be changed by political decree. There will be no school system to alter, no staff structure to manipulate, no party-favoured employee to ease into high office, no national curriculum to impose, and no schools to inspect. Although an incoming government can re-legislate, it would be unlikely to reintroduce the laws and schools of the 19th century. Governments like to be seen moving forward rather than backward even if, in reality, they move not at all!

The new professional personal tutor, working as she thinks fit with her own pupils, will not be appointed by or dependent on any committee. She will be chosen by, and work with, parents and colleagues.

The regional administrative board will enable tutors to do what they are best at: caring for young people. While the regional board will ensure that the law is upheld and children and parents are protected by that law, it will not interfere in a tutor's professional day-to-day work or her long-term agreed programme.

Tutors will find that the system is largely self-regulating, for if, despite the safeguards built into their initial selection and training, some tutors prove to be weak at their job, they will not practise for long because incompetence or lack of interest will see their clientele shrink. If this happens they will have to leave the education service or move into non-tutoring work at a lower salary level where they will find the work less demanding.

The regional board will receive reports from CAVEL and will consider comments, suggestions and complaints that could not be dealt with locally by tutor panel chairpersons or resource centre wardens. Findings will be referred to CAVEL staff who will be required to report back on the action they have taken.

All multimedia lesson material will be available to the public in their homes or community centres, so there will be extensive exposure and knowledge of what is being used in children's education. Much of the reaction to CAVEL material will be parental and will, where sufficiently serious, be acted on by the regional education board.

The board will have other duties. It will supervise the allocation of funds to resource centres and consider the need for new building in areas of rising population. It will project future need, based on demographic findings, both in terms of capital expenditure and tutor and tutor panel supply. It will liaise with the two education stages subsequent to early education and will co-operate in the calculation of future university requirements.

But no committee, local or regional, will come between a tutor and her client. That relationship will be as sacrosanct as it is in other professions. The child-parent-tutor relationship and its confidentiality will be the firm foundation on which the new system will be built and there will be an Agreed National Code for education (ANC) to uphold it. (See pages 141 to 145).

7. Reassurances

1. Fear of change

Untried

Proposals for change, particularly such drastic change as is proposed in this book, will raise genuine doubts and anxieties in the minds of many. When such proposals involve entire nations in a movement away from a long-established school-based system of teaching towards a largely untried alternative, such doubts will be a serious matter and will call for serious attention.

Since 1870 in Britain, and from a similar date in most other Western nations, children have been taught in classes, in schools, by teachers. This has gone on for so long that such schooling is now set firmly in the culture. Even when the weaknesses in the system are at their most glaring there is little desire for any marked change to be made to the basic organisation, and very little at all for the whole system to be replaced by a possible thoroughgoing alternative.

As a result the old organisation is retained, some minor modifications are made to it, some extra money is spent and all is thought to be well – or at least tolerable – until the next crisis threatens. Then the same thing happens all over again, and again, and again.

Even so, doubts about changes which are so drastic that they lead to a whole new system of childhood education are at least understandable, for what is under discussion is the way in which the next generation of children is to be raised in many countries. If mistakes are made, or if the proposed new approaches are flawed, there is no recovering the years children will have 'lost' or the sacrifices parents will have made, or the reputations of the tutors who will have been involved, or the sums of money that will have been 'wasted'. Then, so great will be the disenchantment, that hopes of further experimentation or change will be bleak indeed. The clock will have been set back several decades.

It is therefore incumbent upon advocates of extreme change to offer reassurances and to propose, along with the new ideas, marked caution in their implementation. Advocates have to remember, too, that the Western world is not enamoured of revolution. That world prefers the comfort of 'no change'. It is sceptical or suspicious of those calling for drastic changes in any of the state's major institutions. Education is regarded as one such institution.

Three likely worries about the changes mooted in this book are that:

● Some children, because of their intellectual, emotional and material environment, will gain little from a predominantly home-based education.

- Some parents will feel unable to cope with what they see as the inordinate demands that will be made of them and that they themselves have too little to offer their children in terms of what they see as an 'adequate' education.
- Since the Second World War there have been too many changes in the schools (not too few) and that what is now needed is a period of consolidation and 'normality'.

Reassurance can be given on each of these three points:

First, in the proposal made here for teaching-without-schools, there will be no overnight *coup d'état,* and, vitally important, no pressure on parents or teachers to enrol either themselves or their children or their pupils in the new system. There will be closely-observed trials with volunteer families and volunteer personal tutors and either the scheme will be modified as experience grows, or, if little of merit is seen to emerge, it will be abandoned.

If successful – that is, if the families involved wish to continue their involvement and to introduce their younger children to the scheme, and if other families and teachers approve of what they see and so wish to join – then the plan will grow of its own volition. It can then be instituted in other areas – perhaps with local amendments – to suit the demand. It will gain momentum gradually and peacefully.

Second, much greater recognition will be given to those parents who are already home-educating enjoyably and effectively. It will be shown that, initially, many such parents were uncertain about the wisdom of the steps they were taking in not sending their children to a traditional school, or in removing them from such a school, and were uncertain of their own ability to educate their children successfully at home. In practice, and after many years, most have found that things work well for their children and themselves. Under this new scheme of teaching-without-schools, such families – with additional resources to call on – are likely to do even better. They will be able to show the way to many others eager to join them. The country will be indebted to those families.

Third, to those who feel there has been more than enough change in the schools already, it can be suggested that the phrase *'in the schools'* is highly significant. It is true that over the past 50 years there have been many changes, but those changes have been made *to, and in the schools.* They have not been changes to the school-based *system.* The fundamentals of that system are much as they were 125 years ago and there have been no publicly-announced, fully-resourced and properly monitored attempts made – with a wholly open mind – to devise, initiate and assess the feasibility of the radical alternatives to traditional schools that are now available and which were not even pipedreams to the worthy pioneers of the school-based system back in the 1870s and 1880s.

Decades of *seemingly continuous change in schools* have been disadvantageous in another sense: they have caused people of a reforming bent to spend time debating the latest proposed change to the school-based system and to be diverted, intentionally or not, from debating the much more radical question of *whether we need the schools at all.* A calculating and cynical supporter of the status quo might well assume that if he can keep reformers arguing for years about, for instance, the virtues of streamed and unstreamed schools, they might be kept from asking the far more pertinent question of whether both could be replaced by something far better in a non-school environment.

2. An Agreed National Code

Three parties

Further reassurance to doubters will come via an agreed national code of conduct which will be binding on the three parties involved in early-education. The parties are:

1. Personal tutors and other members of the Professional Tutors' Guild.
2. Parents or guardians of children aged from birth to fourteen years.
3. Central and local government agencies.

Eventually, as with the adoption in the European Community of common laws which affect people in many walks of life, the third party to the contract, central and local government, will be enlarged to become a body of international standing which will represent governments in those countries adopting a teaching-without-schools approach.

The rights and responsibilities of each party will be set out in an Agreed National Code for education (ANC) and these will be incorporated in a legally-binding contract. Each parent, tutor and regional board member involved in the new scheme will sign his or her own copy before benefiting from or participating in the revitalised education service.

Failure to comply on the part of any one party will release the other two parties from their contractual obligations to the defaulter.

Thus there will be no obligation to provide a parent with state educational facilities for his or her child if the parent fails to co-operate in the programmes he or she has agreed to with a tutor; there will be no obligations to retain in employment a tutor whose work is so unattractive that she cannot maintain a personal group of children; there will be easing from office or financial penalties imposed on governors or education officials who do not abide by the terms of the contract and who fail to offer the level of support required and expected.

1. Personal tutors and other members of the PTG

Teaching children without the use of schools will mean for many parents a disturbing change in outlook or expectations and this concern could be carried over to their children. The changes will be more difficult for parents to accommodate than they will be for teachers and education officials. This will need to be reflected in the drawing-up of the national code: tutors and officials must be aware of these parental doubts. There will be many parents who feel the tutorial system has much to offer their children but who, because of uncertainty as to the outcome, will hesitate to opt for enrolment. Therefore, under the code:

- Tutors will explain, advise and reassure constantly, and in this work they will use their professional expertise in parent-pupil-tutor relationships to promote reassurance.
- Tutors will appreciate how deeply-entrenched the school-based system has become in many parents' perception of education, and how difficult it will be for many pupils and their parents to envisage a generation being raised satisfactorily when schools have gone.
- Tutors, especially those who have children of their own, will recognise the problems parents face in the difficult, lengthy, responsible and undervalued task of rearing children and how little ongoing expert help they have received or are receiving.
- The means of establishing effective working relationships with parents and a study of the psychology of parenthood will be fundamental and will feature in tutors' professional training. Tutors will accept that the onus will be on them, as the professionals, to gain and keep the parents' trust.
- Tutors, through the PTG, will publish this three-way code in order to further parental reassurance. They will emphasise the many benefits to be derived from the new scheme if all three parties adhere to the code.

2. Parents or guardians

- Parents will consult a register of personal tutors and tutor panels and gain basic information on a tutor's career, strengths and, by inference, limitations. They will know that the register is frequently updated and maintained by the PTG at the Guild's own expense.
- Parents will be consulted by the personal tutor or panel chairperson on all aspects of their child's study programme and will be given a copy of each approved stage of the programme before it is begun and will then co-operate in its execution.
- Parents will have the right to be present and to make their views known at all formal meetings where their child's progress is being discussed and, at such meetings, will strive to reach a consensus with the other parties concerned.
- Parents will be advised of those areas where tutors feel that parents can help

in the furtherance of a study programme, and of how that help can best be given, and will endeavour to provide that help.

- Parents will have the right to request a meeting with the personal tutor or, afterwards, with the panel chairperson, at any published times or, in emergencies, at other times.
- Parents will have access to an appeals panel if there are serious differences between the parties which cannot be settled at panel or resource centre level.
- On giving reasonable notice, parents will be free to remove their child from a group or panel at any time and to apply for his admission elsewhere, and, on request, will receive resource centre co-operation when doing this.

In return for these rights, parents – and older pupils – will accept responsibilities that will be binding on them as partners in the education process:

- They will support enthusiastically the mutually agreed individual programme of work and help their child with it as much as they can.
- They will make every effort not to involve the child in any differences of opinion that later arise between tutors and themselves.
- They will supervise the working-through of the study programme and will not criticise it in front of the child, and will change it only after agreement with the tutor.
- They will care for their child emotionally and materially in such a way that he can gain optimum benefit from his studies.
- They will ensure the child's attendance at the agreed and scheduled place of study, and will try to accompany the child on some or all of his studies whether locally at the tutor's study or at the local community resource centre, or further away at a national field centre or at a similar centre abroad.
- They will indicate to the tutor any difficulties in the study programme as soon as they become apparent.
- They will heed the tutor's professional opinion on the value of a parentally-proposed course of study and will acknowledge the tutor's right to refuse to tutor such a course if she feels refusal will be in the best interests of her pupil.
- They will meet all reasonable out-of-pocket expenses incurred in their child's education.
- They will accept responsibility for their child's behaviour while he is in the tutor's care.
- They will withdraw the child from a group or panel, temporarily in the first instance, where, in the tutor's opinion, his behaviour is affecting adversely other children's education, welfare or safety.
- They will follow the agreed appeals procedure, and abide by the final decision, finding, if necessary, alternative education for their child at their own expense.

● They will not, while drawing parental salary, take any further paid employment elsewhere.

3. Central (National) and local government

The roles of both central and local government bodies will steadily decrease as the new education system is established, as will their influence. Eventually both will be unnoticeable in the day-to-day work of the other parties to the contract. The governmental role will become that of a major enabler.

The two strands of government, central and local, will have the responsibility of supporting and facilitating the new system in six areas:

● Finance and resource-provision.
● Advice.
● Expertise.
● Arbitration.
● Guardianship.
● Co-ordination.

Finance: from money received through taxation, the government will forward, annually in advance, on a per-capita basis, all necessary funds to resource centre wardens. Wardens will reallocate funds to tutor groups, local field centres, and their own centre's bursar. Government will also finance CAVEL and tutors' in-service needs such as the professional enhancement courses arranged for all personal tutors by the Professional Tutors' Guild.

Advice: government will administer advisory services and, in particular, maintain a central registration system of vacancies in all tutor panels in order first, to help and advise parents, nation-wide, on possible placings for their children and, second, to anticipate future tutor, tutor panel, resource centre and field centre recruitment and the necessary provision of land and buildings.

Expertise: the government will compile, in co-operation with the PTG, a list of tutors, university researchers and authors, from both at home and abroad, who have specialised professional knowledge and who are willing to lecture to or chair seminars for tutors and parents. Neither central nor local government will employ its own inspectors or advisors, but those already in the school-based system who wish to become personal tutors will be interviewed and assessed by the PTG and, if found acceptable, will be offered a truncated course of training and, on successful completion of that, assistance with placement in a tutor panel.

Arbitration: government will be responsible for maintaining local arbitration bodies charged with settling disputes between individuals in the education service. Findings of the body will be available to all at community resource centres, field centres and through CAVEL.

Guardianship: the central government will oversee parental rights in the education service and, should parents be dissatisfied with the help they receive from the PTG, provide them with the required information and advice on further procedures. When necessary it will remind the PTG and local government, through its legal advisers, of their statutory obligations to pupils and parents and of the terms under which they receive state funding.

Co-ordination: the government will co-ordinate all those services needed to help the education service. These will include: health and safety, passing of legislation and tax-raising. It will liaise with foreign governments in the areas of tutor-student training and in the facilitation of pupil, student, tutor and family exchanges in field centres and elsewhere.

3. Changing relationships

The ANC and confidence building

The agreed code will aid reassurance by helping pupils, parents and tutors understand the nature of their task and by providing that task with a framework. It will make clear responsibilities as well as rights. It will do much to dispel the misunderstanding that has sometimes existed in schools between teacher and taught. Schools will have gone, thus allowing relationships between interested parties to be direct, intimate and continuous. This deepening of relationships will be one of the most important and fruitful attainments of the whole teaching-without-schools proposal.

Gradually those elements of the 'instructor' role that remain within the present teaching scene will go. Tutors will be on a par with those professionals in other occupations who regard daily contact with their demanding adult clients as a basic element in their work.

There will need to be radical changes to teacher-training courses. While the psychology of childhood and early adolescence will remain important, the understanding of parenthood and its difficulties as well as its rewards will be a vital addition.

In order to be able to cement sound relationships tutors must be able to talk easily and confidently with parents of all ages and social backgrounds and be able to explain how the new system works and how its potential can be maximised in the interests of their children. It may mean overcoming deep-seated attitudes built up over 125 years: attitudes of 'them and us' and of what 'they' do at school and 'we' do at home – and vice-versa.

The two 'sides' of parent and teacher have been distanced from each other too often and it has been the child, in many cases, who has had to pay the price or learn, himself, how to cross the divide. In the new system there will be no arbitrary divisions between home and personal group. Although in some quarters progress is likely to be slow, it will be possible. With responsibility for twenty pupils or less for a whole two-year period and no long school holidays to break continuity, the personal tutor will have more time, energy and opportunity than her school-based predecessor to use her new knowledge and to improve the relationship. She will be able to set aside several hours on two or three days each week to talk to parents – with or without their children's presence.

An essential ongoing activity that will help the tutor build relationships will be her previewing, with small groups of parents, of CAVEL programmes and study units. Groups will note merits or demerits, see how units fit into individual study programmes, discuss how parents can help their children with follow-up work and, occasionally, compile user-reports for CAVEL's consideration.

Then, with individual parents, the tutor will be able to go through much of the written work pupils have done and clarify notes she has entered provisionally on their child's record. The personal tutor can talk about future study projects and hear about the child's activities at home. She can move conversation on, when appropriate, to promising developments and interests or to difficulties already present or anticipated. Specifics can be debated rather than the hurried generalisations sometimes associated with termly or annual school reports and parents' evenings.

For fourteen years parents will be making decisions, identifying needs, contributing ideas and suggesting changes as their children move through their individual study programmes in their seven two-year stages of early education. They will outline their wishes and hopes. Then, based on these, and with the parent-tutor relationship firm, the tutor will draw up plans for each child heeding carefully what is both desirable and possible.

Several factors will combine to foster good relationships. These will include increased and more flexible consulting times. A professional yet sensitive dialogue with tutors at a personal level in non-institutionalised surroundings will increase parental confidence and strengthen feelings of partnership.

The shorter working week and earlier retirement ages in the developed world will give parents and grandparents more time to become involved in early-education work and will enable their skills and experience to be used to benefit tutor groups. An interesting craft, skill, holiday, journey, hobby or sport can be utilised by tutors as a valuable, different, credible and immediate personal resource in their group work. Increased leisure time and affluence will enable many parents and grandparents to travel abroad and add to their stock of 'useable' experiences.

A duty-tutor will be on hand to help parents, either by a personal visit or by telephone, or fax, or E-mail, with problems that arise during home study periods. When their child's personal tutor is away the duty-tutor, who normally will be a member of the child's tutor panel, will have access to such records and details of current studies as are necessary for her to give sound 'at the time it is wanted' advice.

4. Home as a study centre

Parents will be advised on the provision of suitable home conditions for study and will receive initial financial help with this. Slowly but steadily it will be made possible for children to listen, read and write in an environment conducive to those basic language arts. It will be an environment where sound has significance and where a child can hear himself think. Parents will be advised on study hours, length of study sessions, allocation of study time and the wisdom of allowing some flexibility.

As well as being able to down-load non-copyright material from the Internet, parents will make use of material from their community resource centre and will be encouraged to use all the centre's facilities in their work of getting to grips with the pleasures and perplexities of raising a child. This will reduce further the notion that the parents' own education ended on the day they left school. For fourteen years at least parents will learn from their child's early-education programme because many of the programmes will be taken and studied at home in the course of parental supervision of children's work.

With an increasing use of CAVEL, a pupil's home will become a study centre in itself and will complement the study-area of a tutor's home or the local community resource centre. Eventually, as the new system of education grows and as new houses are built and older ones refurbished, each home will have its own study-library which will become at least as important as any other room, and be essential for the living of a full and happy life.

As home study progresses and becomes more embracing and exciting, the family will, with the help of the personal tutor and multimedia, become society's main agent of learning; it will, in a way, be as it was before school-based learning separated 'education' from the family unit. But it will be immeasurably better. In the 1870s and 80s separation seemed to be the only practical means of extending the child's horizon: he had to be removed from the restrictions of his impoverished home environment and his illiterate or semi-illiterate family.

Now, relatively, the situation is reversed. It is quite ironic that sometimes the restrictions are caused now by the organisation of the traditional school with the *outside* agencies offering almost limitless opportunities for the broadening of childhood horizons. But, eventually, with tutorial and multimedia help, and to the advantage of society, the family will regain its role as principal educator of its own young children.

The tutor's role then, perhaps as early as 2050 or 2060, will be to help with the education of the whole family – several generations of it. By then the tutor will have become a doctor of education: a title full of practical as well as academic meaning. With many existing diseases under control, and much diagnosis and treatment routinely computerised, the tutor's role, status and social value will begin to exceed that of the medical practitioner. Her salary and status will be suitably raised. Perhaps that, too, is less than fifty years away.

Also helpful will be the weakening, on any organised basis, of political and religious influences. Parties, groups, and denominations will be unable to utilise the school system for the promotion of their own ideas and the suppression of others'.

The eternal debates on such matters as streaming and non-streaming, comprehensive or selective schools, opting-in or opting-out, state or private schools, single-sex or co-educational schools, formal or informal teaching methods, phonic or whole-word approaches to reading, will be viewed as historical irrelevancies when seen against the individual child's need for love, affection, care, security, attention, stimulation, variety and long-term interaction with an understanding group of adults and a friendly set of peers. It will then be realised how much valuable time has been wasted over the past fifty years and how many opportunities to help children have been lost irretrievably.

5. "It can't be done!"

Reassurances of a different kind will have to be given to those people who see the many benefits that would arise from an alternative system but who are unable to believe that a new system will ever be put into operation. "It can't be done!" "It'll never work!" "People aren't ready for it yet!" "It's all just a pipedream – utterly unrealistic!" and "We'd never manage without the schools!" are responses that might well be heard. Such people, who might in themselves be willing to give a new system a try but who are doubtful about it ever getting off the ground, have to be convinced that the scheme is viable and imminent.

It is not a pipedream. It is realistic. It can be done. To say to a disbeliever in

148

1999 that, by 2099 there will be no schools, that children and their parents will be given expert help from the child's conception to adolescence with an individualised, tutor-supported study plan for his first fourteen years and that the objectives of all this will be to help such children lead happy, contented, environmentally healthy lives in which they are at peace with their neighbours, will be no more far-fetched than it would have been to tell a citizen of 1899 that within a hundred years millions of ordinary people would earn £250 per week, own their own centrally-heated houses and comfortable cars, go on holidays abroad in aeroplanes travelling at 600 m.p.h., be free of smallpox, polio, scarlet fever and tuberculosis, have the vote – both men and women – at age eighteen, have an excellent chance of a university education and lifelong social security. They would have deemed the teller 'mad' and similarly dismissed his vision as "just a pipedream", and "utterly unrealistic." Yet it has happened: all of it!

Doubters have to be convinced that what is proposed in this book is far less dramatic a change in society than many of those changes that have, in large numbers, recently preceded it. A society without schools is possible and highly likely long before 2099 and the first steps towards that position can be started safely now. The first practical step will be the devising of a credible pilot scheme in one favourable area of the country. This step is outlined in Chapter 8 *A Pilot Scheme.* (pages 151 to 155).

6. Benefits

Reassurance will be needed on the benefits to be derived from teaching-without-schools and it will be desirable to list these benefits clearly and unequivocally. The benefits will fall into four categories in that they will help the child, the parents, the teacher or tutor, and each state which adopts this scheme or one similar to it.

Children will, rightly, be the principal beneficiaries. They will enjoy greatly enhanced personal relationships which will be developed within small, close groups of familiar and intimate peers and adults. They will gain from the emotional and physical security offered by belonging to a long-term, caring and largely home-based personal group where they are recognised, appreciated and important. Children will benefit from the loving attention given by non-stressed personal tutors working alongside parents within a manageable tutor panel of which they will be pupil members for fourteen years. Their powers of learning will be maximised by the appropriateness of an individual study programme made to fit their needs. They will benefit from the mass of material made available by CAVEL and other providers. They will, as they grow older, be more and more involved in the planning of their own work. The state of children's mental health in Britain, which is causing great concern at the time of writing, should improve steadily as their feelings of security within the family, and of being wanted by society, are helped to grow.

Parents, from before the birth of their child and onwards throughout infancy, childhood and early adolescence, will receive as much direct, indirect and dependable help and advice as they feel they need. Both formal and informal ongoing contact with a skilled, experienced tutor who can call readily on many sources of aid will be a boon to those parents who had little preparation for parenthood and who worry, understandably, about the lengthy, difficult, complicated and responsible task they have taken on in rearing a child. They will find that the assurance gained by having someone knowledgeable to turn to, in confidence, at any time, will be immense.

Teachers could gain most initially as they will have the immediate and growing satisfaction of deciding on and arranging their own work and the schedule needed for its implementation. They will have responsibility for their work and be able to relate that work directly to child and parent. For the first time they will be full professionals who can practise free of a school's hierarchical structure with all its attendant stress and restrictions. The energy they save will be redirected to the counselling of their pupils and the assessment of their needs.

The state, as generations pass, will gain by having a more relaxed, interested and contented population. Many existing social ills will be addressed by skilled workers at the close local level of child, parent and neighbourhood. This will be especially so as the benefits of the open-to-all community resource centres, with their wide range of 18 to 24 hour facilities, are fully realised. Each state's employers will gain more adaptable, interested, talented and innovative employees as the standardisation inherent in much of the school-based system gradually passes away. Some of the citizen's personal fears and many of the social and financial costs to the state of unemployment will be assuaged in the 21st century if, through the new education system, citizens are helped to see that there are worthwhile activities in life apart from paid work and that much of that work was, in the past, dangerous, tedious, unhealthy and lacking in any lasting satisfaction.

8. A Pilot Scheme

Five requirements

Voluntary help

A pilot scheme for teaching-children-without-schools will be necessary and should not be expensive or difficult to arrange. The proposal will need, at a very basic level:-

● Seventy or more voluntarily-participating families living largely in one locality, from which can be drawn 140 children distributed fairly evenly within the age range birth to fourteen years. Those children old enough to do so will need to show a willingness to take part. Among the 140 children there will need to be some 20 in each of the seven two-year age bands, the oldest of whom must be agreeable to leaving normal school for at least two years to try something radically different. The children will be guaranteed a return to the school they left, and will be offered additional tuition to make up for any formal examination work they missed should the scheme be discontinued.

● Eight experienced teachers ready to accept secondment for five years in order to practise, after training, as professional personal tutors. In this pilot scheme one tutor will double as panel chairperson and resource centre warden. It is realised that such sample families and teachers are unlikely to be representative of the population as a whole as the sample is likely to consist of those already predisposed to seeking an alternative to the school. But the information gained from such a sample will take the plan beyond the theory and drawing-board stage and give some indication as to whether or not the scheme *would* work, or whether it *could* work if changes to it were introduced.

● A small school – perhaps one due for closure – which will serve as a temporary resource centre.

● Funds, for materials and equipment, equal to the per capita cost of teaching 140 children in traditional schools in that region, plus money for parental salaries.

● An innovative and sympathetic local education committee (and chief education officer) willing to help with the initiation of such a trial in its area. A recent historical example of such praiseworthy innovation is that of Leicestershire County Council in the late 1950s and early 1960s with its readiness to experiment with a two-tier system of secondary comprehensive schools in selected districts of that local education authority. Despite initial doubts in some quarters the experiment became a plan that was extended successfully throughout the county. It worked – and the innovation attracted worldwide interest.

People working in *Teaching Tomorrow's* pilot scheme, in conditions that are far from ideal, will need support. Apart from the initial promotion by a progressive local education authority, attempts will need to be made to attract the backing of MPs and councillors having an interest in education, and also of teachers' unions, university schools of education, educational writers and publishers, parents' and school-governors' organisations, and those bodies who already support home-based learning or flexi-schooling, such as Education Otherwise and Education Now.

The pilot scheme will need to run for at least four years and preferably six so that children can grow accustomed to and enjoy belonging to two or three personal tutor groups. Observation will need to be systematic and thorough, as will the recording of progress and the tentative conclusions to be drawn.

Such a radical and far-reaching plan, one which could lead to the abandonment of thousands of schools, will attract nationwide and, quite likely, worldwide notice. Every care will have to be taken that such focus of attention on a small group of children, parents and tutors is not allowed to interfere with that group's work and wellbeing. It will be for the initiating local education authority to provide protection by limiting, if necessary, media and other access to participants in the pilot scheme: the children and their families and tutors must be given a fair chance if the scheme is to be properly assessed.

Conclusion

But will the plan ever come to pass? Even its pilot scheme? To be quite honest, it is unlikely. The indications are that while Western governments have a desire to see educational standards rise – for various reasons – they see such 'improvement' taking place within the existing school-based system. They seem unable, or unwilling, to accept that while for 125 years the school-based system has benefited some children and parents, it has failed others. Too many governments have seen education as an enhancer of the nation's workforce rather than an opportunity to help individual citizens lead contented, less ambitious, less demanding, less stressful and more caring lives. Few have seen their education system as a major means of promoting peace between peoples, but have tended instead to encourage the spirit of international competition. In the worst cases systems have been used to aggravate differences, boost intolerance and propagate notions of master races: for obvious reasons the time for that is long past.

Gradually, under a teaching-without-schools approach, early-childhood education, like other stages of education, will become internationalised. In building individual study programmes for children and their parents, tutors will be drawing on sources and materials from many different countries. There will be a great and positive sharing of knowledge and of teaching skills, and this will be strengthened by the inclusion in all programmes of study abroad and student and family exchanges. People of one nation will become friendly with those of other nations and be able to understand their way of life and seek out its good qualities. They will appreciate from personal experience, at grassroots level, the many advantages for everyone of friendly peaceful co-existence. They will live in a world unrecognisable from the wartorn, war-weary one of earlier times – of which times the 20th century has provided by far the most horrific, devastating, ruthless, bloody, widespread, selfish, wasteful and inexcusable examples.

Nevertheless, despite all that might be offered by the new system, it would be suicidal for any government to jettison all its schools overnight; but it would be to its credit to run, alongside the traditional system, a voluntarily established radical alternative. The credit gained could be international in the long term. Many Western nations are wealthy enough and have the latent talent within their large populations to make the launching of an experimental alternative wholly practical. A large number of families in the USA and a smaller but rising number in the UK are already involved in alternative approaches and have much valuable knowledge, born of experience, to contribute to any discussion.

Certainly more thought needs to be given to many issues which threaten both the developed and undeveloped world: the environment, the misuse of diminishing resources, employment trends, demographic changes, transport and crime, to name but a few. All these need study and subsequent action which is long term, international and dependent, ultimately, on the use that is made of the power of education.

But many countries are dogged by political electoral systems which restrict such examination to the brief four or five years between government elections. Governments cannot afford to be too unpopular with the electorate at large or with powerful vested interests working within and without the state. Such short terms are inadequate for tackling the huge environmental, social and moral issues that confront the world already, which means that some concensus between political parties within a country and between countries has to be reached at some point. Certainly, changes in governing parties after elections must not be allowed to negate the findings of the previous government's experimental work in alternative forms of childhood education.

But this is *particularly the case* with education where, in Britain for

Figure 17. Three-generation timetable for phasing-out schools.

Decade	Generation	Approximate timetable	
2000	1st generation	Pilot schemes for alternative education with volunteer parents and teachers in one local education authority. Further pilot schemes where demanded.	
2010	Ages: 0 – 70 Years: 2000-2070		
2020		Full assessment of pilot scheme(s) and estimates of demand.	
2030	2nd generation	INADEQUATE 1. Continue with school-based system.	ADEQUATE 1. Introduce pilot schemes into other areas.
2040	Ages: 0 – 75 Years: 2030-2115	2. Consider other alternative systems as ideas and opportunities arise; test same.	2. Extend principle and practice of teaching-without-schools approach. Amend as needed.
2050		3. Improve the retained traditional schools.	Increase recruitment of tutors, make full use of developing technology. Phase out traditional schools.
2060	3rd generation		
2070	Ages: 0 – 80		
2080	Years: 2060-2140		Few people now have any experience of traditional schools:
2090	4th generation Ages: 0 – 85 Years: 2090-2175		such schools are studied as part of Western social history.

example, a child will live through at least three different government administrations before he leaves school at age sixteen, or in the USA where he will attend school through four such administrations. Yet lasting answers to current problems in childhood education will need far longer periods than those. Education is doubly important in that (i) it can help resolve many of the major problems of our time and our descendants' time and, (ii) it can help with the achievement of happiness at a personal level.

In its first role, education provides the means whereby people understand how limited the world's resources have become, how huge are the demands being made on them, and how fragile and interdependent so many of the life-supporting aspects of its structure are. It is in this role of kindly but persistent informant that education is now so important a player. The vast majority of the world's population has to understand what the prospects are that lie ahead and it is mainly through unfettered education that such understanding will come about. Education becomes the world's first social service: if it fails, the rest will matter little.

In its second role it is helping, at an individual level, the attainment of a simpler yet more fulfilling life which will make fewer demands on resources and, at the same time, stand a fair chance of increasing the happiness of each person.

Whether such a double objective can be reached via the current school-based system is doubtful. The present situation is not promising. The whole system, supposedly catering for millions of individual children, is too much geared to the mass production demands of the state and too firmly rooted in the methods and organisation of the past. There seems to be little point in offering the system another generation of children so that it can show what it can do: it has had 125 years in which to do that and few people seem to be favourably impressed by the results.

In everyone's interests, worldwide, an alternative needs to be thought out now and tried, tested and assessed so that in twenty-five years time there will be a viable choice available to those who wish to take it up. This book suggests that one viable alternative is to teach children without the use of schools at all. It could be done, and a start could be made now. Teaching tomorrow has to begin today.

9. Bibliography

Formulating ideas

Eighteen books

The books in this short list are related, in one way or another, to the main theme of *Teaching Tomorrow*. In some cases they are also related to each other as shown in the notes following each title. All have been found helpful in formulating ideas. Readers who are not acquainted with them may find them valuable when thinking about how and why we teach children as we do today, and how we might move on to teach them tomorrow.

Rimmington, Gerald T.: *Education, Politics and Society in Leicester 1833-1903*, 1978. Lancelot Press (Canada).

This history offers a mass of detail as to how arrangements for the education of ordinary children advanced through the 19th century. It is a useful companion to *Teaching Tomorrow* in that it shows how complicated and partisan such progress was – especially in the larger towns – as the nation's social, economic and political climate rapidly changed. Although focused on one city, readers can easily relate events to their own localities. But the book is a 'good read' in itself as it describes well how our current school-based educational structure developed in an age that is almost unimaginable today.

Shute, Chris: *Edmund Holmes and 'The Tragedy of Education'*, 1998. Educational Heretics Press (UK).

A century ago Edmund Holmes was a chief inspector of schools who, for many years, observed the effects a standardised state schooling had on pupils and teachers. On retirement he admitted that much of what he had seen had been of no benefit to children. He wrote his controversial *'What Is and What Might Be'* in 1911, and *'The Tragedy of Education'* in 1921. As Chris Shute says, Holmes's ideas "challenge the foundations upon which modern schooling stands." This is an exceptionally thought-provoking book for all who care deeply about children's education.

Holt, John: *How Children Fail,* revised edition 1982. Pitman (USA), Penguin Books (UK).

John Holt was highly critical of the development of many American schools and what went on in them when he wrote the first edition of his book in 1964 and was still critical in the revised edition published eighteen years later. Much of his criticism was applicable to UK schools and it was – and is – widely read in Britain. Over a million copies of his book have been sold.

Miles, Rosalind: *The Children We Deserve,* 1994. HarperCollins (UK).

Rosalind Miles looks just as critically at parenting and acknowledges the unhappiness of many children in their families. She forecasts no great improvement until society gives "a great deal more thought, time, attention and political will to the plight of children *and the demands of parenting.*" (my italics), and later holds that such parenting cannot be accomplished well "by two overworked parents struggling alone in nuclear isolation." The book gives food for thought in this whole area. Outstanding.

Miss Read: *Village School,* 1955. Michael Joseph (UK).

Kindness, compassion and keen observation of her pupils and their parents, and the emphasis on how the happiness of each party is bound inextricably with that of the other, come through, quietly but assuredly, in this book as the author relates the day to day work of the two teachers in this small 1950s English village school – an institution which may disappear altogether as closure follows closure. This story offers, in its own gentle way, a host of reasons why such closures should cease and re-openings begin.

Davies, Peter: *Mare's Milk and Wild Honey,* 1987. Andre Deutsch (UK).

Set in an earlier decade, this is an autobiographical chronicle of one important year in a rural schoolboy's life as he moves from his small village school to the grammar school of a nearby market town. It is a vital moment for him as he moves on through the school system and, although it relates to a time long gone, (1939), the childhood reactions and feelings described are timeless and universal. What is so available, as well, is the clear indication of the extent to which a child – with siblings and parents – was able to teach himself so much in the course of daily life.

Brooks, Jeremy: *Jampot Smith,* 1960. Hutchinson, (UK).

This novel is about an older age group, and gives superb descriptions of young people nearing the end of their formal schooling and of their continuing education in the out-of-school-hours world. Placed in the middle years of the Second World War, the book is an outstandingly sensitive, all-seeing account of the whole range of feelings experienced by a small group of pupils – evacuated from their own city school – as they move, hesitatingly, through their adolescent years. Brilliant.

Jones, Donald: *Stewart Mason: The Art of Education,* 1988. Lawrence and Wishart (UK).

The ongoing need for children to be exposed generously to the wonderfully humanising influence of music, literature, drama and art, was demonstrated practically by Stewart Mason over almost twenty-five years as Director of Education for Leicestershire. He was anxious not only to give prominence to these arts in the County's schools, but had the vision to re-organise the schools in such a way that the invidious restrictions of examinations such as the 11+ were either removed or weakened significantly.

Jeffs, Tony: *Henry Morris: Village Colleges, Community Education and the Ideal Order.* 1998. Educational Heretics Press (UK).

As Chief Education Officer for Cambridgeshire for more than 30 years, Henry Morris (1889-1961) argued, as early as 1926, that "we must do away with the insulated school" and went on to develop that county's village colleges. These brought to people of all ages the literature, art, music and a variety of recreational activities which he believed made possible "a full life". The author examines carefully Morris's wealth of liberal ideas and his book can be read in conjunction with Stewart Mason's work in Leicestershire (above) and *Teaching Tomorrow's* community resource centres and its strong emphasis on an arts-orientated curriculum.

Mason, Hilary, and Ramsey, Tony: *A Parents' A-Z of Education, 1992.* Chambers (UK).

But not all school leaders – local or national – in Britain or the USA, had Stewart Mason's and Henry Morris's understanding of what children needed or of what teachers could provide if freed and encouraged. Much of what goes on in British education in the 1990s is thoroughly and conveniently documented here in Mason and Ramsey's book and is useful for those parents who use the school-based system in the UK. It is an excellent source of information, but one is left wondering whether the education of our children needs to be quite so complex and bureaucratic a matter as it has become.

Meighan, Roland: *Flexischooling,* 1988. Education Now Publishing Co-operative Ltd. (UK).

Roland Meighan describes some of the main alternatives to such traditional schooling that are available already in Western countries, and his book includes working models. In his *Foreword* James Hemming argues that "it is vital that the alternatives should be explored.." and claims that flexischooling "fits well with the openness and easy intercommunications which will increasingly characterise the way society operates." In many ways it is an apposite companion for *Teaching Tomorrow.*

Mayberry, Maralee et al.: *Home Schooling: Parents as Educators,* 1995. Corwin Press, Inc. (USA).

Some parents in the USA (where upwards of 500,000 children are educated at home) and in the UK (where the practice is growing), avoid the school-based system altogether. Thoroughly researched in the USA, this book throws light on a subject of direct relevance to *Teaching Tomorrow,* and is a helpful, unbiased reference for those interested in home schooling.

Thomas, Alan: *Educating Children at Home,* 1998. Cassell Education (UK).

This carefully and recently researched book is also much concerned with practice: i.e. what is actually being done in the field of home-based education in, mainly, Australia and the UK. It tells of the experiences and findings of 100 families engaged in that work. While the author acknowledges the "immense effort to improve classroom teaching" that there has been, he feels that we have perhaps reached the point at which as much as can be fairly expected from classroom teaching has already been achieved and that there may be no substantial further improvement until teachers are somehow enabled to interact with individual children.

Webb, Julie: *Those unschooled minds: home-educated children grow up,* 1999. Educational Heretics Press (UK).

The author interviewed 19 people – now in their twenties or thirties – who were home-educated for part or all of their 'school' years. She writes: "I wanted to find out what sort of lives they were leading now, and hear their reflections on the process of home educating ... ... believing that discussion of the inevitable difficulties encountered, as well as being helpful to parents and other educators, gives the validity of realism to some generally very positive findings." Her book certainly does that – very clearly.

Nisbet, Stanley: *Purpose in the Curriculum*, 1957. University of London Press (UK).

Whether a child is taught at home or at school, decisions have to be made on *what* he is to be taught: what selection is to be made from the mass of material to hand and the subsequent content of any agreed curriculum. Here the author examines the subjects traditionally taught in schools and evaluates each against a sensible set of relevant criteria. Although his book was first published over forty years ago, much of what Nisbet has to say is as pertinent now as it was then, and that speaks volumes for any book on education!

Butler, Dorothy: *Babies Need Books*, 1980. The Bodley Head (UK).

The author is firmly convinced not only that children are learning from birth, but that such learning is enriched by the enjoyment of books from babies' earliest days. This book is full of sound, gently-given advice on how – as the publisher's introductory note puts it – books not only "entertain and comfort, but stimulate the imagination, stir the emotions and help to forge relationships." She bears out Nisbet's and others' high evaluation of the teaching of literature.

Cass, Joan: *Literature and the Young Child*, 1967. Longman (UK).

So does this book which offers parents and teachers of children aged approximately two to eight years a wealth of insight into how they can enrich those children's lives through literature. In her introduction to the book, Sybil Marshall notes that if the imagination of all little children could be nurtured as the author suggests, many might suffer less fatigue, pain and distress, and most would, hopefully, live happily ever after.

Baker, Carol: *Getting on With Your Children*, 1990. Longman (UK).

This author ends her brief but wide-ranging and reassuring book with: "Our children are on loan. We must enjoy them while we can and help them to become the best they can be." This is not only an appropriate ending to Carol Baker's book, but it could be for the readers of *Teaching Tomorrow*. Her book would make an excellent discussion document when considering a personal tutor's work with younger children in this 1999 teaching-without-schools proposal.